M000234926

The Drama
of the Rite

Worship is the act of simultaneously throwing
oneself open and offering one's self up.
Gabriel Marcel, *Being and Having*

The Drama of the Rite

WORSHIP, LITURGY AND THEATRE PERFORMANCE

Roger Grainger

sussex
ACADEMIC
PRESS

BRIGHTON • PORTLAND

Copyright © Roger Grainger, 2009

The right of Roger Grainger to be identified as Author of this work has been asserted in accordance with the Copyright, Designs and Patents Act 1988.

2 4 6 8 10 9 7 5 3

First published 2009 in Great Britain by
SUSSEX ACADEMIC PRESS
PO Box 139
Eastbourne BN24 9BP

and in the United States of America by
SUSSEX ACADEMIC PRESS
920 NE 58th Ave   Suite 300
Portland, Oregon 97213-3786

All rights reserved. Except for the quotation of short passages for the purposes of criticism and review, no part of this publication may be reproduced, stored in a retrieval system, or transmitted, in any form or by any means, electronic, mechanical, photocopying, recording or otherwise, without the prior permission of the publisher.

Personal names throughout the book have been changed.

British Library Cataloguing in Publication Data
A CIP catalogue record for this book is available from the British Library.

Library of Congress Cataloging-in-Publication Data
Grainger, Roger.
The drama of the rite : worship, liturgy & theatre performance /
    Roger Grainger.
    p. cm.
Includes bibliographical references and index.
    ISBN 978-1-84519-306-5 (pbk. : alk. paper)
1. Liturgics. 2. Public worship. 3. Theater. 4. Performing
arts.
I. Title.
BV178.G73 2009
264.001—dc22
                                              2008029924

Mixed Sources
Product group from well-managed
forests and other controlled sources
www.fsc.org Cert no. SGS-COC-2482
© 1996 Forest Stewardship Council

Typeset and designed by SAP, Brighton & Eastbourne
Printed by TJ International, Padstow, Cornwall.
This book is printed on acid-free paper.

Contents

Foreword by the Right Reverend Dr David Hope

Roger Grainger has a passion for liturgy and this is nowhere better illustrated than in this present work, *The Drama of the Rite*. And the clue to his passion is well stated in the title, namely that he well understands quite rightly that liturgy is no dead letter, but rather a living and life-giving action. It is a drama into which all who gather for worship are inescapably drawn.

But then, here is no ordinary drama, here is a drama which draws all our human selves and relationships into the abundance and profligacy of the life of the Blessed Trinity. Worship is that action which makes us who and what we truly are – sons and daughters of the eternal God who came among us in Jesus Christ – where already past and future are celebrated in the present of liturgical time. Thus Roger Grainger writes – "The action of *seeing the future in the context of the past* has a transforming effect upon the present."

Roger Grainger explores with great understanding and learning the concepts of rite and ritual in relation to liturgy and brings also his rich knowledge both of psychology and theology to enliven what might otherwise be a somewhat dull and dreary discussion; and always his observations and suggestions are grounded in possible practical applications for any and all who participate in worship. Thus, for example, he commends and gives ideas for 'liturgical' workshops which can then easily and readily translate into an altogether deeper and more profound experience of the transcendent and transcending power of worship.

In describing the Eucharist as 'the prototypical' Christian liturgy, Roger Grainger does not either ignore those 'rites of passage' which have a particular significance both for the individual and for the community as well as society as a whole. Here he cites well-recognised authorities such as Mircea Eliade and Arnold van Gennep, relying somewhat on the latter to set out his reflections on Christian Initiation, marriage and death.

In all, here is a book which reflects considerable learning, yet is written in a very attractive and accessible style. It takes us to the heart of the Christian mystery, to that place and time which we call worship, where the vulnerabilities, weaknesses and failures of our human nature are at once embraced and transformed in the abiding love of the eternal God.

Commendation by the Archbishop of Canterbury, Rowan Williams

Rituals change people; that's what they are for. A ritual that works as it should is the embodiment of a story, so that the participant at the end is not where they were at the beginning. And in the Christian context what changes people is the relationship God creates with them – so that Christian ritual is the embodiment specifically of how relationship with God in Jesus Christ draws us forward in healing and reintegrating the fragmented stories and selves we bring to it.

Roger Grainger has written extensively on liturgy in the past, and in this brief but weighty new study he spells out some of the ways in which this pattern works in our practice. The discussion is both theoretically sophisticated and practically pastoral, with examples of how the liturgical transformation of individual and communal experience can be worked out in a variety of circumstances. At the heart of the argument is the conviction that liturgy, so far from being some kind of impersonal formality for the life of the Christian community belongs in fact with the most genuinely personal dimensions of Christian life.

This is a book of carefully distilled wisdom, valuable both for the student of liturgy and for the Christian, lay or ordained, seeking to understand the central role and enormous resourcefulness of liturgy for that constant conversion which is the life of faith.

✝ *Rowan Cantuar*
Lambeth Palace, Petertide 2008

Introduction

. . . the skin of Moses's face shone because he had been talking with God. (Ex. 34, v. 29)

We have always been told that we should begin at the beginning and go on until we reach the end. This is the way we deal with the business of living which requires a certain attention to procedure. In one sense, therefore, it is true of liturgy when we see it as the story of our relationship to God and one another. We remember how our story began (or must have begun, we think) and look forward to its eventual ending in terms of its completion, something which will make a kind of eventual sense as a message about ourselves and the way our life has gone.

Because it is about liturgy, however, this book starts in the middle. Liturgy is an event in itself, a statement of truth which breaks our rules of procedure and consequently lifts us out of ourselves to share in what lies beyond us – and to do it *now*. Liturgy is an epiphany; or at least, this is what it is intended to be. Regarding liturgy then, we start with the unforgettable experience which gives it birth and enshrines its meaning in timelessness, an experience lying at the heart of liturgy and of those who perform it.

This feeling of meeting transcendent truth, encountering God, is fundamental to our identity as worshippers, being the core of our shared Christian story. All that this experience embodies, all that it has meant and will mean, is the central fact of our worshipping together, its motive power and driving force. We may be anxious, self-obsessed, disillusioned, semi-convinced by our own and other people's more liberalistic and 'down to earth' way of looking at what we sometimes call the real world; but in liturgy we "suspend our disbelief" and seek to open ourselves up to what would otherwise be unimaginable.

I make no excuses for putting it like this. At the heart of our worship is our intention – our *need* – to meet God and we use liturgy to do this. To meet him we must be changed in the attitude of our hearts and minds and in the messages conveyed by our actions. This is the central truth of liturgy, and why we do it at all. Certainly it is responsive action on our part – but it becomes a willing response, a personal intention. From the point of view embodied in liturgy, change takes place at the heart; our heart, the rite's heart. Forms of worship are put together by human beings, of course; but the intention to do this does not originate with us, nor does the joy expressed in the words we say or sing together and the movements and gestures embodying them. In liturgy we reach out for God's joy and the finding is in the seeking. The action itself is one of a shared meeting, and in it we encounter the One we are seeking.

Or else we have nothing to share. Our experience holds within it both past and future. It enshrines the knowledge of an original consummation. Each liturgy is therefore a rebirth into joy. This is a truth about worship itself. Certainly we are very conscious of not always remembering it, certainly of not feeling ourselves able to live up to it. We are painfully aware of a tendency not to rise to the occasion. We come to worship trailing our uncertainties and inadequacies behind us, and are reminded of what we have forgotten: the flame of life which is ours, its source and meaning and purpose, what our ancestors called its *end*.

This is what I mean when I say that we really begin in the middle. As we shall discover later on, the action of performing a liturgy turns upon the experience of joy, the joy of transformation which lives in its central movement. This is the point of balance between beginnings and endings, past and future – the everlasting present. It is a moment which gives momentum, bringing us face to face with the reality which allows us to be real. There is a good deal in what I have written here about the structure of liturgies: how each has a well-defined beginning, middle and end. The purpose of this, however, both in theory and practice is to focus on the central encounter with God. This is a transforming event, even though we may choose not to regard it as such . . .

Perhaps this is not as judgemental as it sounds, however. It may be that we are not always in a position on any particular occasion to respond in the way we might otherwise choose to do. Liturgies are not compulsory epiphanies: things get in the way, we get in the way. We choose to suit ourselves; it is our dubious privilege. Yet all who come to worship have a reason for coming, or at least the memory of a reason; something that is powerful enough to turn us in a particular direction, away from ourselves towards the heart of the matter, the source from which the choosing self draws its ability to choose at all.

Ritual, then, carries with it an option for deliverance, an opportunity to lay aside the burden of freedom in a timeless moment of surrender. We are led out of ourselves to a meeting with God who calls us into a richer, more devoted way of living and dying. Liturgy is a path to follow, a mountain to climb, a bridge to cross. Above and beyond all else it is a setting for an occasion of mystery – the profound mystery of what it is that lies beyond and outside the self. The mystery of *otherness*, and of how we relate to it.

> In all its manifestations, the relationship with the other is a relationship with mystery. (1987: 75)

So Emmanuel Levinas put it, whose own life was almost entirely devoted to asserting the urgency of our own personal need to acknowledge realities outside ourselves and beyond the scope of our urge always to be in control of the people and situations we come across – what he calls "the egotistic spontaneity of the Same" (1969: 43) which seeks to homologise all its experiences in order to make sense of them. Philosophically speaking, the only way to come to terms with the fact of otherness is by abandoning the attempt to contain it within our usual way of 'thinking things out': the other is beyond us *by definition*; its very beyondness draws us to it . . .

And this is how we experience God in our lives, as the Other draws us to Himself. Nowhere is this expressed more vividly than in our liturgies. Liturgy is not the only way, nor the first time, that we meet God – but it is an action in which we involve ourselves in full awareness of his intention to transform us by leading us away from ourselves in a very specific and practical way, as liturgical action is put together from the evidence we have received, both as individuals and communities, of his loving and sustaining relationship with us – memories, assurances, epiphanies of the Other abiding here, in the invitation to draw near.

Draw near. So far as we are concerned, this *is* the liturgical action. Our thoughts and feelings, everything we know and have known, our awareness of being ourselves in fact, are symbolised in his gesture of responsiveness and the pledge of mutuality it embodies. 'Draw near' is the way in which we encounter God, leaving ourselves behind as we concentrate on him. At whatever point in the service the words are said, the liturgy itself is the transforming event, the heart of the mystery; which is what I mean when I say that liturgy lives in its central wholeness – our self-forgetful meeting with God.

This book attempts to bridge the gap between writing theoretically about liturgy and actually finding a way of making our own worship more immediate and authentic as the expression of our actual lives, our own experience of God and one another. Part of it is based on 'liturgy workshops'. These are informal ways of exploring those aspects of our personal awareness – memories, hopes and fears, feelings about ourselves and other people – which we want to bring to God in our worship in as expressive a way as possible, thus giving life to liturgy 'from the inside'. Those used to a lifetime of more staid worship may be alarmed by this approach; not for long, however, as the aim is to encourage us to explore what it is that we ourselves bring to the liturgy we love so much and have grown used to over the years. Because they are not actual services, they can be adapted to take account of any nervousness we may feel about 'getting involved in drama'. The real drama, of course, is the liturgy itself . . .

Getting to the Heart of Things

Liturgy is about making time in our lives for God.
Making time and making room.

To look at time first. In liturgy we give God 'the time of our lives'. We often talk about giving someone *quality* time. In a very real sense, worship is just that: a distillation of our use of the time available to us whereby we devote it to the purpose of worshipping God. We take a period of time – minutes, hours, days, in some cases the intention of an entire lifetime – to concentrate together on God.

Worship uses a special form of language, which we call ritual – or in its written form, liturgy. It is special because it is designed to refer to the spiritual significance of the things which happen to human beings. Liturgy refers to human life, its past and future.

Liturgy refers to the past and the future. It recounts things that have happened 'before' and repeats promises about what will come 'after'. It does these things now, so that their meaning is brought into the present in order to change it for us. This is what is meant when it is said that liturgy "takes place in eternity". The action of *seeing the future in the context of the past* has a transforming effect upon the present. It is as if we lay hands on time in order to open it up and find out what it is about. In liturgy we stop time in order to take a closer look – not experimentally, as if we were setting out to find some kind of scientific and rational answer to our problems in living, but joyfully and wholeheartedly, as those revisiting times when we have been most aware of the presence of God in our lives, and his purpose in our lives – moments of fulfilment, perhaps even revelation.

Another way of saying this would be that liturgy takes place between past and future so that the things which happen in it can jump both ways. It has often been said that liturgical symbolism points in two directions at once, past and future, seen and unseen, earth and heaven. Thus, when we move into liturgical mode we pass into betweenness. Each act of worship is a vantage point, a hearable, seeable, moveable mountain top for looking outwards on time and eternity . . .

In this sense all acts of worship happen in the meantime, which is the interim between events and a time of opportunity for what-ever is new and unknown. The past had brought us this far; it is up to the future to take us onward. Now, however, we have slipped outside the flow of time and present ourselves – not as unoccupied, because human beings can never be that and stay alive in the world – but as engaged in being ourselves in time to meet God *between* our various businesses. We come because we are called. The liturgy calls us to meet God. This is not surprising – we are used to regarding it as his liturgy, believing that in some way he is enshrined within it, and comes to meet us out of it; it tells his story, or the story of his dealings with men and women like ourselves. This may sound prim-itive, but it is what we feel, however we may choose to describe the feeling, and we are concerned here with the way we feel as well as think. This is a basic fact about liturgies. They involve whole people, not just parts or aspects. Spirit, certainly – but flesh too.

Liturgies, then, symbolise the meeting between God and humanity, just as the presence of Christ in our sacramental litur-gies shows forth the relationship of human and divine. Art is used as a symbol of perfection, the timeless being of God. From this point of view liturgy's main concern is with timelessness; eternity in a time-framework. The assortment of materials assembled for creating an act of corporate worship is deceptive; much more is involved than the collection of bits and pieces. Within this assem-blage of spare parts a pattern is hidden which will only really emerge when the rite is performable and performed, an experience familiar to those who put acts of worship together anywhere in the world. Liturgy stands forth as a language for God not because of its raw materials but its construction; not the things it is made of but the way it is made.

As a potter moulds clay into the shape of a vase, or as Spirit gave form to the waters of chaos, so the worshipping community creates liturgy. We cannot manage perfection, but we can symbolise it in the way we arrange our imperfections, both in skills and materials. Because it involves bodies, liturgical art is fundamentally kinetic. Sometimes it moves spatially, but it always moves within the dimension of time. It is the way in which it uses time that fits it for its unique purpose as a symbol of wholeness. Liturgies point beyond themselves and express perfection within themselves by means of the way they make progress in time. Their actual shape corresponds to Euclid's perfect number because they are in three parts which in itself gives them an iconic balance, a pointer to perfection. But their purpose is not to be left like this as the mathematical sign for an abstract completeness. Rituals are meant to be worked through; their perfection is in the progress they make and help us to make with them.

Liturgies are intended to be whole statements, not tentative suggestions. No-one speaking about God can say everything to be said, or even everything they themselves want to say. A liturgy asks God's permission (and help) to speak on God's behalf by inviting him to say what he wants to hear *through* it. Called to be definitive, liturgy sets out to speak as definitely as possible. This is why they are arranged the way they are, with a beginning, a middle and an end delivering their message in three parts, each part reinforcing what the others have to say, climaxing in the final authoritative, clinching statement. "What I tell you three times is true," Lewis Carroll's Bellman says, and he learned it in church (1876).

This kind of final authority needs space for expression as well as time for expressing itself in. As well as setting time aside, liturgy makes room for action, just as it is a matter of space out of time, so is it also a matter of time out of space. Liturgies set time aside and make room for things to happen. Time and space together express intention and provide opportunity. Practically speaking the second may actually take precedence over the first, in a sense being the trigger for some kind of liturgical action – however strong our desire to worship God together, we need somewhere to do it; recognising a suitable location provokes the impulse to use it precisely for this! This is not as far-fetched as it sounds. The relationship between space and expressive action has been remarked upon by semioticists and students of theatre for many years now; emptiness requires to be filled in some sort of specifically transformative way; its expressive potential resists being wasted.

That is how it seems, anyway. Like any other kind of nature, ours abhors a vacuum. Here we see the principle applied to the interaction between things – in this case, places – and the people who use them; our relationship with the world we live in, the circumstances of our own lives as human beings. From the very beginning of our worship together, space is our context; it is part of the reality we are expressing by reason of being part of the way we express it, which leads straight back into liturgy, whose characteristic medium now turns out to be not time and space – but space as the way in which time and eternity express themselves.

We use space in three distinct ways, the most obvious of which being the room our bodies take up when we meet for worship together. Next, we talk about it, to one another and to God, describing actual places (our own and other people's experiences in and perception of them) and using them as metaphors of the intangible and unlocateable (e.g. 'The City of God'). Lastly, we use space in a physical, geographical way as an analogue of somewhere else, particularly when we might respond to the invitation to come forth in faith and receive the body of the Lord by moving out of our seats towards the altar table, something which involves more than a simple physical manoeuvre. This last is the specifically liturgical use of space, and the one which we shall be concentrating on in the workshops included in this book.

From the very earliest times, men and women have used space in this way as a metaphor for spiritual processes; measurable distance as a symbol of non-measurable progress. Archaeology suggests it, anthropology describes it, the history of religion explains it. 'The rites of passage' documented by Van Gennep (1960) and Victor Turner (1974), and explored by generations of field workers, depend on the human impulse to express mankind's embodied reality in acts of worship which are moved, as well as thought about and yearned for – to show our relation to God as we understand relationship to be, moving through what we know as our reality towards the unknown reality awaiting us. As we progress through the world, so we change and develop spirituality; what better metaphor of our passage than these familiar landmarks.

Because our life journey is such a powerfully spiritual metaphor for us, the places in which we represent it take on a particular significance, the importance we associate with place of worship – churches, temples, mosques, gurdwaras, etc. In a sense, this is always a holiness by association rather than that of the encounter itself – it is the 'meeting with God' which transforms us rather than the place where it happens. Just as the intention to worship God creates its own time, the metaphor which sees him at work in our lives makes its own space. Liturgy happens wherever, and whenever we allow it to be fanned into flame, using whatever is to hand to give it its distinctive character and application. Time may seem more flexible than space – but space itself turns out to be no more rigid than our own imagination will allow it to be. Wherever two or three have room to relate, liturgy comes to life. Like drama, it first of all makes its own world, then transports us beyond it.

This is a book about the emotional and personal content of liturgy. It is as much about group experience and group workshops as the kinds of church services we are used to thinking about as liturgy. It contains workshops rather than actual liturgies, being mainly concerned, not with the service itself but with what it is *for*. This is because I believe the heart of liturgy is to be discovered not in words and movements, but in what motivates these things – what gives them their immediacy and life. Rituals which fail to be personal become ritualistic or even just boring; and if these rituals are intended to bestow shape and meaning on the course of ordinary living, dullness and impersonality are their worst enemy, or almost their worst.

In fact liturgy's principal handicap is the appearance of venerability without any discernible relevance to what is actually happening in the lives of the people performing them; the kind of liturgical activity which passes for worship but does not manage to invoke or create any sense of a God recognisable outside the archaic liturgical aims themselves. The worst thing that happens is that the wrong God addresses us in our worship – the God of ecclesiastical holiness, of sacred tradition – instead of the God who is here happening among us.

A good deal of hard work has been put into recent efforts to revive the worship of churches who possess written liturgies by making these more adaptable at the level of their surface text. Official liturgies have become more varied with regard to the versions of traditional material available, and there is more scope for individual congregations to decide on the detail of their worship. Whether this has succeeded in breathing more life into the experience of shared worship is a matter of debate. Only a certain degree of change can take place in the underlying structure of the rite without lessening its capability to express the transforming action of God in the way it is designed to do: its power to be itself, to be *liturgy* rather than any other kind of human statement about the meaning of life and death.

Any change in our worship which is to be real must take place in our own ability to use liturgy as a message addressed to God, a place and time into which he welcomes us. The change must be in ourselves rather than other forms of worship; we must learn again how to think and feel liturgically. The basic outline of liturgy is simple and direct. The emotions and ideas it represents are profound, however. When people re-discover what liturgy is for, they recognise its life-giving potential where they had formerly felt either boredom or a mild aesthetic excitement.

At first sight, certainly, there seems to be considerable difference between liturgies and workshops. There is certainly a difference, but at the deepest level there is actually no contradiction. The one leads naturally into the other, and is only really fulfilled by it. I have found that a liturgy workshop flows naturally, sometimes even spontaneously into a liturgy. This can happen whether or not the group decides to move out of the workshop space into the worship area (or out of the church hall into the church itself.) Such relocation is entirely appropriate for the final phase of a liturgy workshop, and represents the kind of movement into higher ground which lies at the heart of corporate ritual – it is splendidly liturgical and very moving too!

The workshops are a training place for the quality of involvement required in and deserved by genuine, authentic participation in liturgy. The importance of this cannot be over-estimated. Liturgy is an open and public expression of where the Church itself stands in its relationship with God. There is a great deal about 'heartless' religious ritual in both the Old and New Testament, but liturgies do not have to fly in the face of God's demand to the extent of those excoriated by Amos and Hosea* in order to fall short of their true authenticity and purpose, which is to proclaim his glory in as unmistakeable a way as possible. Even half-heartedness and staleness are a failure in mission.

If our rituals fall short it is principally as the expression of meaning – the delivery of a clear, unmistakeable message about God and humanity. Without this they cannot but appear unintelligible. Freud links religion with neurosis – 'unadaptive' behaviour having no rational purpose – by saying that religious people give an appearance in their rituals that they do not actually know what they are doing, and what it really is that drives them to behave in such a way: "How often the petty ceremonials of religious practice gradually become the essential thing and push aside the underlying thoughts" (1907). A Christian worshipper's "underlying thoughts" are about God. It is a great shame that the fact is not more obvious.

Making time and clearing a space for God. Not such an easy thing to do on anything like a systematic basis. The experience of trying to say our own private prayers certainly brings this home to us. So far as worship goes, it is being with one another in God's presence: the way that the feeling of his presence spreads among us, catching hold of our attention and centring it upon him. But the task of concentrating definitely grows much harder when we have set times and places aside especially for this purpose.

Harder to achieve, and consequently more pressing: familiarity breeds contempt, as they say. Having to worship in this way can have a disastrous effect on human spontaneity – as the priests of the Jerusalem temple discovered to their own cost and the disdainful fury of the Prophets! Giving God the space and time needed for corporate worship on anything like a regular basis is a problem for Christians everywhere; and not only for Christians. All organised religions share the same challenge, that of balancing attentiveness

* E.g. Amos 5: 21–24; Hosea 6: 6.

and routine, freedom and structure – or at least their own unique version of it. They must do, because it is an essential part of being human.

In other words, it is part of what we are offering to the God whom we worship. Our shared acts of praise and devotion are things *we* do, actions *we* perform, and our difficulties in performing them express who we *are*; not only yearnings and aspirations but failures of concentration and distractions are evidence of our actual identity. From our human point of view they are the raw material of what we bring to God. As Christians who set out to worship the God and Father of Our Lord Jesus Christ it is essential to bear this fact in mind, because it is, quite literally, crucial. To spell this out even more clearly, the worth-ship which we are offering to God is Jesus's, not our own.

Perhaps we know this, but we always need to be reminded of it when we are considering the value and significance of Christian worship: that the mind-blowing worth it represents is a gift we share with one another because we are sharing it with God – and doing so at his invitation.

Our offerings of worship are acceptable because he makes them so. From our point of view they may sometimes be less beautiful than we would like, less polished and refined, lacking in the skill which would express our appreciation of the divine perfection. However, it is not as simple as that – thank God! Of course we should do our best to express our perception of God's beauty and holiness, showing in the process our own innate understanding of what holiness and beauty are and can be; but we should never fall into the trap of confusing our own work, however amazing this may be to us, with the God who inspires it. This is really what the Bible writers have in mind when they see God saying 'I hate and despise your feasts' (Amos 5: 21). Losing concentration, so that our minds wander and we forget what we are really supposed to be doing, or it becomes mechanical through over-use, are secondary considerations.

Liturgies are really there to stop our minds wandering and direct our attention to the business of worship. Our Christian liturgies express and show forth God's acceptance of us, and his transformation in and through Jesus Christ. We shouldn't be either too ashamed or too proud of them, but we have every reason to take delight in what they mean to us and say about us. They are always special occasions. Any problems they present us with are caused by their unique importance in our lives as Christians.

For they are unique. Being a Christian is intensely personal. In fact, it is as personal as anything could possibly be. This doesn't mean that it is a solitary occupation, however. Even those who live by themselves, either by choice or circumstance, are not spiritually isolated, being surrounded by a 'great crowd of witness'. It is not possible to be fully human – or even human at all, according to some psychologists – without experiencing the presence of other people, either seen or unseen. Liturgy is worship which is focused on relationship with God and others. In full awareness of one another we address the God who is with us. Our experience is personal and corporate. In fact, it is all the more personal *because* it is corporate; we are called to share . . .

For Christians this fundamental experience of shared humanness is particularly intense because it is God's way of revealing himself to us. We are "members of the body of Christ". One body, many members. As individuals we are only complete because we participate in him. Participation is our way of being; God in person has shown this to be true, and we acknowledge its truth by loving one another 'in his name'.

So Christian worship is essentially a corporate action and remains so however few or many are gathered together, this is because faith itself must always be something shared. Christians are those who heard the good news and were consequently "united by faith with those who listened" (Heb. 4: 2). Liturgy is the public proclamation of a uniting faithfulness; as such it lives on at the very heart of the Christian Church. For human beings all meetings are important because the action of making contact with other people refreshes and renews us. This is more than that, however. We don't simply meet to share ideas and feelings or make plans for the future. Drawing near by faith we concentrate on a shared relationship with God which is the most important thing about us. We meet to rediscover who we are.

Because this is so very important, so vital to the way we are in the world, it has an immediate effect upon the way we perceive reality. You could visit this in several ways, one of which would be to say that worship's subject is eternity, so that it cannot really be understood in time-bound language; and the same is true about space too – it is too effectively taken up with this world's spaces to be of any use as a way of measuring transcendent things, however conscious we may be of their actual existence. We can use language certainly, but only because of its ability to point beyond itself. To use ordinary words and phrases to demonstrate their own limitations and so pay indirect homage to what lies beyond.

Time and space are different, however. They don't depend on our descriptions in order to exist or to give them the particular shape they assume for us at any one time. The human faculty involved here is that of *spiritual imagination*. We all possess this, but there is a tendency for us to undervalue its importance. Because of the pressures exerted by the necessity to think and feel, to respond in a practical way to the demands of life, we often neglect this special, personal ability to reach out and make spiritual contact with things which can't so easily be tied down. This, again, is where other people give us courage to trust our own yearning for spiritual fulfilment as we join with them to lift up our hearts to the God who is both so near and so far off: immeasurably far off, as near as life itself.

Perhaps I should say something here about what I mean by 'spiritual imagination'. This is the ability, which we all possess, of thinking about the significance of things we are familiar with and take for granted. Perhaps it is a bit more than this, however, because it includes the ability to value things because they are felt to be true without being completely understandable. This kind of imagination is more about not knowing than knowing; or at least the kind of knowing involved reminds us of the kind of journey in which we carry on rejoicing in what lies ahead. We haven't arrived, but for the meantime we carry on journeying. Perhaps there will be moments of refreshment or even of rapture – there is no suggestion here that it is only hope which beckons us on – but we neither plumb depths nor scale heights. Neither here, nor yet . . .

The scientific imagination needs to know more, of course. Its spiritual counterpart is better at exploring ways of being a person than establishing facts about the world. It is both more daring and more ordinary than dispassionate observation. Its most tangible expressions are works of art and religious liturgies, both of which plainly state their concern with the literally impossible before they go on to demonstrate the uniqueness of the spiritual truth they embody.

This book is intended to encourage those taking part to think, feel and work together in this way, calling on their spiritual imagination. The liturgical frameworks on the other hand are an invitation to people to try out a particular kind of art form associated with liturgy throughout the world. It is really a form of *public poetry* and needs to be approached like this – precisely and with discretion so that word and meaning fit together in as expressive a way as possible. We do not have to think of ourselves as playwrights to do this, but as people who are searching for the best way to say what we really mean, in the way we really want to say it. Certainly we can, and do, use other people's words to do this, if we feel that they express what we personally think and feel. After all, this is the time-honoured way in which to create acts of worship. To use Lévi-Strauss's expression, worshippers are pattern-makers (he calls them *bricoleurs*): they use all kinds of ideas and materials to express a yearning for contact with divine perfection (1969: 50–52). When we ourselves set about making or performing a liturgy we are like the householder who "brings out of his treasure what is new and what is old" (Mtt. 13: 52). This is the drama of worship.

In this book I have tried to show something of the relationship between drama and worship in the short liturgical outlines that crop up from time to time, which are partly acts of worship and partly drama workshops. Certainly they are not intended to be taken as actual liturgies in themselves, but as illustrations of the way people can work together to create genuine liturgy, liturgy of the most refreshing and also vividly personal kind. Worship is multi-faceted and takes many forms: planned and spontaneous, complex and simple, its form governed by circumstances but its intention always the same – to make the best possible statement about the most important relationship of all, that between God and humanity. Worship is characterised by the wholeheartedness with which it attempts to carry out its purpose; it is its intentionality which allows us to call an act of worship a rite – a corporate action embodying a single purpose. Intentionality gives worship its distinct shape, as a series of linked actions and ideas from which all suggestions of randomness have been excluded. Genuine worship presents us as actively engaged in what we are saying and doing. This and not anything else is what we really mean, and we want to express it as well as we know how. This is its ritual quality; its value as a definite statement of meaning and intent. It may seem presumptuous to describe the ideas sketched out here as *rites*; but such is their underlying aim. Consequently it is in fact what they are, at least in embryo.

Rite and Drama

Liturgy's purpose is to have a transforming effect on the lives of those involved. No wonder, then, that its action is dramatic in the sense that it resembles an actual piece of theatre. In this chapter we shall begin to look at some of the ways in which liturgy and drama make use of the same kind of interpersonal structures of action and reaction. Ritual and theatre have this in common: that they counteract the human tendency to include otherness within the self by regarding it as an idea to be woven into the pattern of thought, filed alongside every other idea, and treat it as a real presence – the presence of a beckoning absence, a gap which can only be filled by personal relationship, the experience of reaching across to the Other.

Liturgy is a *kinetic* medium 'expressing itself via the relations between the motions of bodies and the forces acting on them'. At least, this is how we shall be regarding it here – not as an excuse for re-shuffling ancient texts with a view to re-arranging them in a more scientifically historical order or even translating them into more up-to-date language. The kinetic identity of liturgy requires individual examples to be treated holistically, as greater than the sum of their parts, communicating their meaning as individual dramas. The liturgical scenario is both extended and focused; in other words it functions like a language, by means of the relationship between its various parts, each word meaningful in itself but surrendering its individual sense to that of the sentence. Liturgical sense is a unity in itself; to divide it up into separate words and phrases, gestures and movements is to risk misunderstanding it. Liturgy does not simply *use* language; it *is* language, of a direct and forceful kind, congruent with its own subject matter. It is an exceedingly honest way of communicating truth.

From the point of view of this book, then, liturgy is something which is performed, not studied. This is a worshipper's book, concerned with the exploration of shared experience rather than the examination of texts. Liturgy creates its own world which means that it is not really intelligible except from inside that world. It manages to bypass the attitude of mind which believes itself to be capable of making all things intelligible, and only succeeds in missing the point of so much it claims to understand. If it instructs, it does so through involving us in its own processes and addressing us in its own language. Most of the time, however, it enjoys and celebrates a relationship rather than teaching a lesson. Cognitive understanding is drawn from it rather than discovered in it. For the time being we live out what is happening to us instead of trying to analyse its significance – as, of course, we do in all kinds of drama.

The structure of liturgy encourages a quality of relationship between persons which other kinds of organised interaction either underestimate or ignore altogether. Liturgical structure takes account of how, when and where we perceive ourselves as existing, and the way this affects our relationship with others – particularly the Other. This after all is what worship is about. As we have seen, human worship depends on some kind of setting, some recognisable position within space and time, which are both factors which affect relationship through their influencing upon human attitudes. It is personal encounter that creates liturgy, revealing it to be a way of healing the emotional wounds which we sustain during the course of our daily lives, and which we tend to regard as involving other more private and personal aspects of our relationship with God. However, worship and pastoral care can only be academically separated, what we reveal about ourselves in the company of our fellow members of Christ's body is no less intimate than what we share of ourselves in the privacy of our own homes. Liturgical sharing can be more wholehearted in fact, because of the courage it lends us to visit places in our thinking and feeling to which we normally deny ourselves access, just as self disclosure, despite sometimes causing us embarrassment, frequently brings with it a degree of relief in the resolution of repressed conflict and the release of pent up feelings. Liturgy speaks with authority as a drama, requiring more than a temporary or provisional assent, because its reality is actually superior to our own. We are the players, and God himself our *metteur en scène*. It is these things we have to consider first of all as we look at the liturgical symbol as the means whereby we communicate with God, calling upon all our capability for demonstrating what we perceive, not merely thinking about it. Above and beyond anything else, liturgy is a sign of engagement. The action of reaching out which it embodies is a characteristically human action, expressive of human purpose. This is what the word itself actually means: "the people's work". What you do, says Christ, you must now do in remembrance of me. This is the primary reason for liturgy. It is an action of corporate responsiveness, a gesture of engagement, a form of address. In addressing God we engage with his world. We see him in terms of his presence in the world. This could be interpreted in many ways, implying either greater or less involvement, spoken and written language being particularly skilled at making such distinctions. Liturgy however is less ambiguous. Whatever words appear to spell out, gestures are unmistakable; there is no escaping the fact that a corporate liturgy, like any human gesture, aims at making contact in the most direct and immediate way of which we are capable.

Thus the truest thing about liturgy is also the most obvious: that it is something we do on purpose to make contact with God. It is the sign of a purposiveness which is both individual and corporate; the intention of individuals, communities, the entire human race – in this sense it is something which should always be undertaken afresh. This is why we, like the Old Testament prophets, are so offended by stale, half-hearted worship, which we say God feels the same way about as we do. Each liturgical act should be offered to God as something addressed directly to Him, some new gesture of love, thanks, needfulness, penitence, praise . . .

Obviously such a thing can never be permitted to become automatic. If the work of liturgy depends so much on the commitment it signals, it will certainly need to be taken more seriously, both with regard to what it says and the way in which it says it. Those embarking on liturgy should have some knowledge of the sea on which they must set sail. The rite itself begins with a call to attention (and a warning of the dangers of shipwreck!); but we may be used to such warnings and custom has caused us to take them for granted. Perhaps custom has had the same effect on the rest of the liturgy as well, so that its importance as a jumping off point, an initial gesture of commitment, a signal of willingness to engage, has begun to fade. If this is the case, perhaps it needs attending to – working on – before it gets any worse.

The argument of this book is that the best way of working towards greater involvement in liturgy as a living human experience is to explore it. Actual liturgy comes to life only within a particular setting, namely one being used as a context for worship. The uniqueness of liturgy is brought home by an examination of the particular ways in which ordinary space and time are regarded within corporate ritual; its way of reproducing this concrete symbolism under the entirely different conditions necessary for working experimentally with other people is the measure of its ability to refresh our sense of the mystery which lives at the heart of genuine liturgies, those which are able to serve as opportunities for the healing of wounds and transformation of lives.

Liturgy is about embodiment. It speaks of the spiritual in the language of concretion and makes invisible things tangible. Some have considered this to be a crude approach to matters of value: how can the movement of bodies express the subtleties of thought and feeling? Certainly if truth is a matter of winning or losing arguments, liturgy's dependence on movement, sound, colour, the three dimensional presentation of human environments, might limit its relevance, presenting it as a distinctly crude way of entering into conversations about intimacy. By itself, however, the cognitive–emotional paradigm is very far from being a useful way of approaching human truth – and if it is unable to deal truthfully with the human, what use is it as a language for speaking honestly with God? Human experience is inescapably embodied; to some extent our bodies are always with us, even when we can no longer actually feel their presence – so that to be honest about ourselves is always at some level of consciousness to be aware of embodiment.

So far as relationship with God is concerned this is a crucially important consideration; the possibility of having such a relationship depends upon it. For us, relationship involves the individuality of those who are in relation. Without this separation between persons we lose our individual outlines and are confused. The factual presence of the human body, its unyielding this-ness and here-ness makes this kind of merging impossible to contemplate in any realistic way, so that however feasible it may be theoretically it always manages somehow to *feel* wrong. Our inalienable individuality perceived in our own physical presence gets in the way and prevents us from denying the facts about ourselves. Apart from anything else, liturgy reminds us we are not divine.

Working together in liturgy by involving ourselves personally in what we are engaged in doing has the effect of bringing home to us the limitations and advantages of the bodies which we depend on so much in order to be our own recognisable selves – and yet so easily overlook in our characteristic pre-occupation with abstractions. The embodiment of experience is a major objective of liturgy which sets out to explore human awareness of space, time and relationship in terms of the interaction and juxtaposition of actual human beings, not simply ideas about them. Our involvement with one another proclaims a deep need to be changed by God's Holy Spirit; just as we open ourselves to one another, abandoning our privacy in order to share, so the rite opens us up to God. Because they depend on willingness to reveal personal experience in order to change it, liturgies act as passage rites; that is they embody an awareness of the significance of time and place for people engaged with the process of making spiritual sense of human existence.

Liturgies demonstrate eternity's ability to transform time. They function as rites of passage because of their ability to transform personhood and so change human existence. This power to give form to experience as well as celebrating important stages attained in the course of a clearly marked journey through life widens the scope of liturgy and shows it to be much more useful than people tend to think it is. Used like this liturgy acts as midwife to personal experiences and inter-personal situations which, although deeply felt by those concerned, remain too vague – or too specific – to be acknowledged as social fact. The outlines presented here are meant as models for liturgies tailor-made for an entire range of occasions rendered unique by the form in which they are celebrated. The liturgies themselves might be as carefully crafted or as spontaneously put together as circumstances dictate, for the fact remains that however limited your skill may be, so that the result may seem crude when compared with better established service orders, it will nevertheless prove equally effective, simply because of its liturgical shape.

The extreme simplicity of this rite of passage, and its ability to transform incompleteness into a definite statement, is one of the main reasons for my writing this book. If liturgy is capable of intervening in our ordinary ongoing experience and presenting us with this kind of statement about where and when our life is situated – who we *are*, in fact – it is obviously an essential tool for living, and one which we would be foolish to ignore; if it can do so simply and effectively, then our neglect of it is hard to understand, unless we have a special reason for restricting its use. Perhaps we have handed it over to those specially set aside to monitor the ways in which it is put together and carried out; perhaps its extreme simplicity and availability make it potentially dangerous if it falls into the wrong hands. It could certainly change things, because that is what it exists in order to do. As far as the Christian Church goes, its more inventive exploration as a means of expression by those 'on the shop floor' of the Church is surely something to be encouraged.

In liturgy, as in drama, meaning and shape belong together very closely indeed, because the order in which the events, ideas and feelings described follow one another in liturgy requires the same care as that needed for any record which we wish to present as clearly and vividly as possible. Paradoxically, the story form itself adds weight to the message it carries. This is a principle clearly set forth by Aristotle in his *Poetics* (Butcher 1951): that a story may be true or false, fiction or history, but the fact that someone has taken the trouble to put it into the form of a story brings home its importance to those telling it. This is because the events described and the way in which they are presented reinforce each other, as the shape of the narrative focuses the things contained in it, their immediacy standing out against a background of order and their liveliness given weight by the formality of the presentation. Above all, liturgy is about *intention*: the intention to worship God in the most expressive ways at our command. The occasion may be, and often is, unexpected, but the result can never simply be 'ad hoc'. On the contrary, the emerging liturgy should always aim to be genuinely custom-made, as the act of worship we have designed it to be.

Ritual and Symbol

The way in which 'drama-which-knows-it-is-drama' helps us to make emotional sense of what is happening to us in our ordinary lives – what we call 'real' life – is by giving a transient event – the "three hours traffic of the stage" as Shakespeare called it – a universal reference. In other words, role-play takes on a timeless significance, a truthfulness capable of transcending the succession of events. Liturgy, however, already has this because of its nature as *ritual*. The drama sets out to portray life, while ritual mirrors the perfection of the Infinite. In this sense then the real subject matter of ritual lies beyond the everyday experiences of living – the subject matter, that is, not its effects as we are drawn into the sphere of beyondness by paying it attention with our whole selves in acts of worship.

Ritual, then, far from being an empty repetition of meaningless gestures, which is what it is often taken to be, is the archetypal language of religious awareness. "A phenomenon can qualify as 'religious'," says the Dutch anthropologist Meerten ter Borg, "if it helps people to come to terms with their sense of being finite by seeming to transcend human limits" (2007: 1). Religious ritual, then, is reflexive rather than descriptive; its subject matter reflects a glory which cannot be directly accommodated within human awareness.

There are several ways in which our worship may reflect the perfection it is trying to convey. To begin where we are, with the people we know, ourselves in fact, Aidan Kavanagh reminds us that "Every liturgical act is the assembly succumbing to *logos* revealed" (1990: 93). By *logos*, he means the Word incarnating divine perfection, the very being and meaning of God; and he goes on to say that it therefore follows that "One should engage in liturgy so that attention is called to *logos* rather than to one's own virtuosity" (p. 94).

The fact of the matter is that if one is seeking to demonstrate the wonder of one's own creativity and the skill one possesses in embodying this in complex and inventive scenarios, then one has obviously lost the point. Ritual *involves* us, but it is not primarily *about* us. It is certainly not about our cleverness. Nor is it about our virtue either, by which I mean not only purity and moral excellence, but ability to cope with situations of trial and testing, ordeals to be overcome by which we demonstrate our prowess. These dangers and difficulties are intrinsic to the rite and must be so if it is to be a way of telling the truth about ourselves; but our impulse as worshippers is not to dwell on the point as if in some way it reflected glory upon ourselves.

Because ritual is about God, it must be personal. It must respond to the God we meet person-to-person. As Christians we acknowledge this in all the ways we think about God, claiming that our sense of his being personally involved in our lives, and we in his, is the final and original truth about him. He is to be known as Person and our relationship moves us to reach out to him as friends reach out to one another. His Presence among us proves this. It is not something we thought up for ourselves.

Ritual is about God – a personal response to a personal response. It is, in Charles Williams's phrase, the "salvation [which] lies everywhere in inter-change" (1937: 248). This means that it will possess certain characteristics essential to a meeting of persons intended to be an expression of the love which is between them.

1 – *concentration*. The rite will concentrate on what it is doing in expressing love. It will not be distracted from this, and every part of it will bring home this message: I am about love. Whatever other subject is brought up will serve this purpose. This leads directly into

2 – *singleness of mind*. Those taking part in the ritual drama must treat it as of vital importance to their personal situation, setting other concerns at a distance, or at least trying to do this. The nature of

ritual as the proclamation of something of ultimate significance helps us to 'suspend our pre-occupations'.

3 – *focus*. This is a characteristic of the rite itself, corresponding to 'singleness of mind' on the part of those involved. The various sections of the act of worship correspond to a clear statement, a gesture which the congregation makes away from itself towards the Person they are addressing, and to whom they are listening. The intention is to move into the spiritual, away from the distractions of the real. This requires focus, allowing what is seen to become a vehicle for the unseen.

4 – *intentionality*. The rite expresses our returned human purpose to worship God, drawing near in faith to the source of our being. The rite itself conveys this intention, but as a human creation it cannot function without our endorsement in the form of a real movement on our part to answer his call. The rite cannot function automatically by itself. It is always evidence of a deep involvement in our past to address God in this way.

5 – *shared spirituality* – a sense of awe associated with involvement in the rite; what Rudolf Otto isolated as 'the numinous' expressed imaginatively in the artistic shape of the rite and experienced as a visiting transcendence, drawing us closer to its source as life responds to Life. Such a thing is difficult to describe except in the language of the rite itself. However it is blessedly familiar to all who lose themselves in liturgy.

6 – *congruence*. So the rite is a symbol of healing for the spiritual wounds which divide us from one another and also from ourselves, divisions of an inter-personal and intra-personal kind. To focus on God as the source of our healing is in the deepest sense of the phrase to come clean about ourselves.

7 – *poetry*. This implies something which is not merely the attempt to be expressive, but – to adapt Coleridge – "the best words" (movements, sounds, gestures) "in the best order". This involves careful selection of materials in order to communicate a special kind of message in a particular kind of way, so that form marches with content to be as explicit as possible. It means leaving things out as well as putting things in, paring the message down so that it is simple and precise, its meaning as unmistakeable as you can make it without extraneous information. There is a paradox,

here, of course, because the more we keep unnecessary material out, the more meaning we actually allow in, because of the ability of poetic expression to point beyond itself to what may be perceived by the mind and heart but not precisely described, our most sensitive encounters with the truth, what Wordsworth called "thoughts that lie too deep for tears". There is nothing in the rite which is only literal; the whole is:

8 – *metaphor*. Poetry differs from prose because it is always metaphoric; its use as poetry makes it so. Metaphor provides us with a way of expressing what would otherwise be inexpressible. Speaking of precious stones, Marlowe talks of "infinite riches in a little room" (*The Jew of Malta*, I.i.36). He could very well have been describing metaphor, not simply using it. Metaphor has the ability to point in two ways at once. It carries us along with itself by using the things we do know as pointers to what we cannot grasp – or can't grasp yet. The more familiar the things it uses, the more powerfully do they assume the 'mind-blowing' meaning-beyond-meaning which metaphors are capable of pointing us towards. Within the context of spiritual relationships, when the subject transcends our ability to describe in literal terms, metaphor becomes our principal means of expression. This is why those who use the language of religious ritual, the special code of meanings that are essentially metaphoric, choose their words carefully and their movements and gestures in order to bring home that everything taking place within the context of the rite is therefore a way of reaching out to transcendence. Ritual itself is an acted metaphor, directing us towards whatever it images, through the power to reach beyond the prosaic which is a property of being human, a skill which in fact we all possess if we choose to make use of it; the skill to point beyond skill. The ritual metaphor renders the entire rite:

9 – *symbolic*. Although religious ritual may use spoken and written language it does not depend on this for the delivery of its message; the entire ritual action – its nature as both statement and metaphor – proclaim a message in themselves, one which ties together the various meanings and messages which have gone into creating it and gives them the impact of a single statement about the relationship between God and humanity. Words, movements, gestures transformed into an action of total worship, which because

of its symbolic shapes, says more than anything it itself contains, has a meaning which resists misinterpretation – the shape of an encounter with the divine. The simplicity of this fundamental act of human worship, its absence of elaboration and explanation says more about God's holiness than words or arguments which, because they are what we normally use in order to make sense of things, so easily persuade us that we are capable of dealing whith what Rudolf Otto designated "the altogether Other". The gesture is always the same – the simple, whole-hearted avowal of human reality in contrast with God's glory. When the Dinka tribesman described by Godfrey Leenhardt ceremoniously tied a knot in a corn-stalk this wasn't in any way to remind God to send rain; no, it was to remind *himself* that he had made an act expressing his trust in the relationship which existed between them. The same is true of all genuine liturgical actions, however complex and skilful their outward manifestations may be. The magnificence characterising some Catholic and Orthodox ceremonies serves the same purpose. The worship abides in the symbolism – in bestowing a symbolic intention upon the ordinary. If what we do is meant to be symbolic in this sense, it will correspond to what Ricoeur calls "A primordial sign of the sacred" (1971: 216).

Concentration; single-mindedness; focus; intentionality; shared spirituality; congruence; poetry; metaphor; symbol. These are all characteristics of religious ritual, each one affecting in one way or another the state of mind and heart of those putting acts of worship together and also the men and women who will be taking part in them. All are important requirements for involvement in authentic religious rituals.

A final characteristic of ritual is clearly connected to its symbolic way of working. This is the extended metaphor of *narrative*. Because this is so very fundamental to liturgy, it deserves a separate chapter.

IV | Liturgy and the Shape of Story

At a level which is fundamental and immediate, plays and liturgies are related by the way in which they tell their stories. Story-telling involves the description of some kind of process involving a change which takes place between two states of affairs: 'before' and 'after', the change having taken place during the time encompassed by the length of the story. Because of the importance bestowed on this change, a story can be seen as a description of an initiation into a new state of affairs, *i.e.* the 'after' state. Fictional narratives can be and are used as templates for changes, or – more importantly – ways of making human sense out of developments in people's lives which otherwise run the risk of seeming meaningless and arbitrary.

Stories are used to make sense of changes in human life. At the same time, the basic story form may be used in different ways to fit situations which are themselves different and call for their own particular kinds of approach. The variations involved may not be concerned with what happens in the events portrayed, but with the significance attributed to the way in which they are being 'worked through'. Similarly, the personages involved may be of differing social ranks or occupations. They do not need to be 'of high estate' for the story itself to have particular meaning; indeed, human ways of discovering meaning permit a story to make its point more effectively if there is scope for real change of any kind – emotional, social or spiritual. More importantly, actually being in the story renders its characters 'special' and gives them a value and significance which eludes them in 'real life' (which, of course, is the principal reason for telling stories in the first place!).

This value-bestowing property of story renders it particularly appropriate for messages about human values, specifically the recording of events prized for their intense significance both to the personages within the story and, by implication, the people reading, listening to or otherwise sharing in it, who allow themselves to be imaginatively gripped by the events which are taking place in it. We shall be looking at some examples of this, concentrating on the way that content and form interact in some well-known stories. What binds these narratives together is the way in which they have all to be consciously shaped, with a beginning, an ending and a climax in the middle. What separates them is the extreme variety of human situation shown, each of them recognisable, or at least imaginable, with reference to things which actually happen to people and animals.

First of all we consider two scenarios which are very well known indeed, the first a fairy tale, the second a bible story. They have been chosen *because* they are so familiar, and also because the characters involved provide such a dramatic contrast. Jonah's life – and that of the Ninevites – is radically transformed by the direct intervention of God himself; Cinderella's by the magical powers possessed by her fairy godmother. In fact 'Cinderella' has been chosen for its lack of sophistication – what some might regard as downright banality. They would be wrong, however; it is because the story is so very 'corny' that it is so powerful. Over the years its impact has actually increased, as all sorts of associations have grown up around it – memories of childhood, the excitement of 'going to a real theatre'; the presence of dearly loved people and adventures carried out in total safety – a world of fantasy rooted in domesticity which is real and recognisable. Far from making the change involved seem less drastic, these things render it all the more impressive: as striking as the contrast between the Prince's palace ballroom and Baron Hardup's kitchen. In an important way, this story is improved by those elements which seem to detract from its credibility, as these are highlighted in the pantomime version, which is the way we know it best: in Buttons's buffoonery and the absurdity of Cinders's Ugly Sisters.

The story is actually made more, not less dramatic by introducing these 'rubbishing' elements because of the contrast between the trans-personal significance of such an amazing change, and the very obvious limitations of the people actually involved. This again is something fundamental to the way in which drama and liturgy bring home their message. It explains, for instance, why Shakespeare intersperses his most dramatic and moving moments with episodes of comedy which distract our attention, leaving us unprepared for what is to come. In theatre, tragedy and comedy are used to reinforce each other. From this point of view the story of Jonah is presented more straightforwardly; but then its subject is an explicitly religious one, and it is offered as historical narrative, not fiction. This distinction also applies to material which is liturgical. It stands for the vital distinction existing between theatre and liturgy at an epistemological level: *the way in which we believe the story being told.* Some stories have, at some point or other, been invented although the point which they intend to make remains true; others embody truths about being human which are ancient and profound; others still are true in the sense that we believe the events they record, or things substantively like them, actually took place. Certainly, few people are likely to admit to believing 'Cinderella' in that sense, although it certainly presents us with a striking image of the way in which someone's experience may in fact be transformed by events totally unforeseen!

Cinderella (Originally Chinese; collected by Perrault)

Once upon a time, long ago and far away, there lived a young girl. She was called 'Cinderella' because it was her job to look after everyone and keep the house clean and tidy. Her father, an impoverished nobleman, had two other marriageable daughters, both of them exceedingly ugly, whereas Cinderella was not ugly at all. However she was not considered to be important either; and when, one day, there was a Ball at the Prince's palace, her father sent his two elder daughters along in all their finery, because the Prince was a bachelor. Cinderella, however, sat alone in the kitchen. She longed to go to the ball too, but she had no suitable clothes to wear and no means of getting there, either. Suddenly, out of the blue, an old woman appeared before her, introducing herself as her fairy godmother. 'I've come to get you ready for the ball', she said. She sent Cinderella off, all ready for the ball, on one condition: she must return home on the stroke of midnight, or her splendid clothes and coach would vanish. At the Prince's ball, Cinderella is the most beautiful girl there. The Prince is entranced, asks her to dance with him, and falls in love with her. As they are dancing the clock begins to strike midnight – and hearing it strike, Cinderella runs out from the ballroom, leaving the Prince amazed and distressed.

Back home in her kitchen, made infinitely more depressing by its contrast with the ballroom, Cinderella sits alone once more. However, in her haste to get back while the clock is still striking she has left one of her shoes behind her, so that as she sits there in the kitchen the Prince is searching the entire kingdom to find the person to whom the beautiful shoe belongs. Arriving at Cinderella's father's castle he is shown her two ugly sisters, who are both quite sure it will fit them. However it is much too small for their large feet, but just the right size for Cinderella's small one. So she and the Prince are married, and live happily ever after.

'Cinderella' is an exceedingly well-known story, but it is only one story among the infinite number which either do, or could, exist. What all these tales have in common is that they all have the same shape – the shape they must possess if they are stories rather than merely accounts of things which have either happened or been imagined happening. It is quite simple to invent a story, using either actual events or events that you have made up in order to create a story. Story-making is a characteristic of the human mind. Nowadays it is considered a proper subject for our most serious attempts at understanding reality (Sarbin, 1986). Moolie Lahad (1994), a psychologist who makes therapeutic use of the story making which plays so great a part in the way we live our lives, divides stories into six parts:

1 The main character, and where he or she lives.
2 The mission they must carry out.
3 The person (or creature) who will help them.
4 The obstacle (or traumatic event) which stands in the way of the mission's completion.
5 The way this is overcome and the situation transformed.
6 The end – or is it? (adapted from Lahad).

Applying this to the Cinderella story we have the following:

1   Cinderella is introduced as living at home with her father and ugly sisters.
2   She is unable to go to the ball.
3   Her fairy godmother arrives to enable her to do this.
4   At the height of her happiness, as she dances in the Prince's arms, the clock begins to strike midnight and magic goes into reverse.
5   The shoe fits, and the Prince recognises her as the girl he wants to marry.
6   They marry, and this story has reached its conclusion.

At an even more basic level than this, the story is in three parts rather than six: Parts 1–3 belong together, as do Parts 5 & 6, leaving Part 4 at the centre of the action. Looking at it this way, we are very much aware that the story is, both literally and metaphorically 'about' Part 4. In other words it concerns what happens when tragedy strikes and an insoluble problem is encountered. This particular tale comes across to us as a light-hearted version of the human reality in which stories exist in order to help us come to terms with problems and situations; however the point is more seriously made in a story like that of 'Jonah':

Jonah, a servant of God

Jonah, a servant of God, is instructed by Him to warn the people of Nineveh that they must repent of their evil ways. He sets out, but instead of heading for Nineveh he takes a ship for Tarshish, in the opposite direction.

On the way, the boat he is in runs into a fearful storm and is in danger of sinking. Discovering this to be Jonah's fault, the sailors throw him into the sea. Jonah is rescued from drowning by a large fish sent by God to save him. Inside the fish, Jonah, believing his life to be over, prays to God for help. The fish spews him out onto dry land which turns out to be Nineveh. Jonah's plan to escape his mission has failed completely, but having arrived he sets about converting the city's inhabitants. He does this with some success, Nineveh being quite different from how he

expected it to be: Finally God uses Jonah's bush he shelters under to bring
home the inclusive nature of His own love for men and women.

There are obvious similarities between Jonah's story and the tale
of Cinderella. Both protagonists start off in situations in which they
experience personal difficulty or hardship (exploitation and abuse;
being ordered to undertake a dangerous mission), and both find that
things get markedly worse (being forbidden to go to the ball; being
thrown out of a boat in the middle of a storm). Both are given help
in their difficulties (a fairy godmother; a large fish), and both are
brought to a place where life collapses in on itself. The fish's belly,
the world at a minute past midnight, are vivid images of the chaos
at the place and time when worlds collide; and the new life awaiting
heroine and hero 'on the other side' chimes with the culmination of
all authentic stories, where 'the end' means 'purpose achieved',
instead of just signifying the last of a chain of successive events.

Cinderella's story is a fairy tale, the subject matter for a
Christmas pantomime. Jonah, on the other hand, is a treasured
biblical text, one mentioned by Jesus himself. Despite this, their
purpose is the same; to describe an occasion when total change
broke into a human life, disturbing its course in a way which
prevented it from ever being the same again. Presented in story form
these occasions become exemplars of and for our understanding of
such changes, which we call transformations. This is how we
perceive this kind of revolution-in-living, the kind of circumstances
we expect to find when we hear about it.

To look again at the story of Jonah, the most obvious thing about
it is that it has a very definite turning point, where, in the belly of
the fish, Jonah turns to God and says: "I am driven away from your
sight: how shall I look again at your holy temple?" (Ch. 2, v. 4) The
story orders itself in the most striking way as a kind of journey or
progress up to and away from this point.

A: The voyage
B: The fish's belly
C: The Arrival

The drama which is implicit in this sequence stands out clearly
in theatre of all kinds. Many classical dramas reproduce the story

shape over five 'acts'. Later plays telescope the action into three parts in order to end each act in a way which is structurally significant (*i.e.* 'dramatic'). Consequently, Act I ends with the climax of the play's exposition: this is what the play will be about; Act II concludes with the major crisis, an event which is shown to be irreversible and final; Act III celebrates a reversal of fortunes and its ending signifies the final closure of the play's action. Thus the problem to be solved or situation to be dealt with at the beginning comes to a crisis at the end of the first part (A), causing desperate measures to be taken, often involving or suggesting some kind of journey, actual or metaphorical, away from the threatening situation. In the second part (B) things get worse, erupting in a different kind of crisis, one which is totally unexpected, so that this section ends in what appears to be total defeat. In the last part (C) what seemed failure is shown to be success of some kind – *i.e.* the Classical Greek *metanoia* or reversal of fortune. A well-known example of this schema, taken at random from the Shakespearian canon would be

Julius Caesar

A: Acts I and II. This is the story up to Caesar's death, a situation rising in tension, the audience having been told what is going to happen . . .

B: Act III. Caesar is assassinated. There is civil turmoil and political chaos.

C: Acts IV and V. The alliance against Caesar falls apart, and Octavius and Antony restore civil order and the stable rule of the Caesars.

A more modern example, again at random, would be Edward Albee's '*Who's Afraid of Virginia Woolf?*'. Albee actually provides titles for the three acts which make the shape even more obvious.

A: Act I: 'Fun and Games'
B: Act II: 'Walpurgisnacht'
C: Act III: 'The Exorcism'

The troubled game-playing of Act I gets badly out of hand in Act II, ending in domestic disaster and breakdown of relationship; a new, sadder but wiser life emerges in Act III. It is the shape represented by the acts which matters, not the act division itself. Thus, in Sophocles' *Antigone*, which is not usually divided in this way, the crucial tragic blow, when Antigone is finally dismissed by Creon, falls at line 885, roughly two-thirds of the way through – that is, at the end of what would be Act II in a three-act play.

We have been looking at stories and plays in order to discover their basic shape, the order of events which transmits an underlying message about human transformations – that they do not simply happen, but do so in contrast to whatever was already taking place. Plays and stories enact the shape of real human change, seen diagrammatically as the relationship between 'A', 'B' and 'C', where A is the starting point, B the intervening reality, and C the final destination. This is not a straight forward movement, beginning at A and ending with C, otherwise B would be an unnecessary addition to the schema. In fact, B has a particular role to play in allowing C to follow on, by clearing a space for it to happen; in this way C is able to signify an authentically new state of affairs, qualitatively not just quantitatively different from what went before.

In the language of the story and ritual, the problems whose solution is achieved at the end of the narrative become most extreme at its mid-point. Here at the crux there is nothing but the problem, none of the factors which made it avoidable earlier in the story remaining; there is nowhere to go but into an impossible situation, trusting that a new way forward will somehow be made available. Put like this it is easy to see that the mid-point is the pivot on which the action turns, the moment of self-transcendence which allows ceremony to, in Clem Gorman's phrase, "lift us onto higher ground" (1972: 45) – here, at the story's centre is the pivot on which the lever rests, allowing it to function as a way of shifting obstacles in its path.

Such is the power of story and its ritual enactment. It depends upon its underlying shape, which turns out to be not A→B→C, but actually A↔B↔C, as both beginning and end find their real meaning at the centre, where the transformation takes place. In this sense, story and rite move inwards towards the centre before moving outwards towards an expression and declaration of new life. Without this turning point a narrative, whether it is read, told or acted, is merely a record of events, and a church service simply a recital of prayers, readings, spiritual songs, which expresses devotion but falls short of delivering a clear message about the relationship it celebrates. In practical terms this means that in order to be itself, Christian worship must be able to articulate the Christian gospel as this is concentrated on Christ's sacrificial act. The story of Christ is the story of Christians, and the Cross is both its form and its content. Mention the Cross, and the story of our own birth, death and resurrection falls into place around it so that we have a genuinely Christian liturgy. The central message is there, but we are free to spell it out in detail; which is where our liturgical skill, our ability to put a service together, comes in.

In liturgy the 'shape of three' and the reality of spiritual transformation belong together. At the heart of liturgy is a point which is neither here nor there, a directionless state of affairs which we must live through but cannot dwell in or on – the presence of an absence in which no-one may stay but all must visit on the way to somewhere else, somewhere on a higher plane than before. "Touch me not," Christ says to Mary Magdalene: meet, but do not grasp.

"Worship transports us into the heart of God". Stephen Platten's words describe the experience of those who refresh themselves at the source of all relationship. In worship we lose our self-consciousness and throw ourselves into the arms of love; and as long as this remains our intention and purpose we are able to forget, or at least suspend our differences, even those which characterise our daily experience as human beings and know a timeless, placeless moment of truth:

"Our hearts are restless until they find their rest in you."

Of all the things theatre does which remind us of its liturgical origins, the most important perhaps is its space-making function. Theatre encourages us to change because it is a place made for change to happen – a place where, through the reality-expanding, spiritually transformative power of symbol, change *can* happen; a place where we learn to speak in a new way about the possibility and presence of change as we discover the language of metaphor and allow our souls to sing. Not alone, however; the soul does not sing by itself. Describing human creativity, Martin Buber speaks of a particular kind of responsiveness as the source of art. This, he says, depends upon "The unconscious humility of being a part of participation and partaking [which] is the true food of earthly immortality" (1961: 113). In acts of worship art transforms space into an opportunity for responsiveness; in this place, at this time, God and the heart sing together:

> "I had been struggling with myself so long to cope with loss and loneliness, when the consultant found signs of cancer and suggested I had chemotherapy. When she said this I don't think I felt anything at all."

Joan's testimony made the point clear:

> "It was Saturday when they told me, so that when I came to the Parish Eucharist next morning I was really only half alive, just going through the motions. I thought I might as well go and stand with the choir because that's what I do. Then we started to sing the first hymn and suddenly I was alive again. Suddenly my heart lifted 'Lift up your hearts'. Well, you can say that again!"

This kind of thing happens spontaneously in acts of worship; but the action is not entirely automatic. When we feel ourselves addressed in so personal a way we respond wholeheartedly, totally, to the impulse to praise, losing ourselves in the action of "running into our Father's arms". The impulse of self giving and surrender which gives our soul wings is the gesture which makes us artists. It is the same gesture, the identical movement of being whereby we lose ourselves in order to rediscover ourselves in a different place altogether. We give ourselves to the action of co-operating with what it is that is calling us. It is the gesture of co-operation which is the work of art.

The work itself may be considerably elaborated, of course, not always to the advantage of the original impulse, although even the most pedestrian work of art shows some vestige of the original responsiveness which gave it birth. Responsiveness of this kind turns out to be contagious, "inspiring and blessing" (as Buber says) all who come into contact with it, passing on its genius from hand to hand, sometimes powerfully, sometimes very subtly, always potentially renewable, in accordance with the terms of its original responsive gesture in which the human soul is called on to open itself to the life of Otherness.

Those who believe in God are consciously aware of the source of this liberating experience. Needless to say, artists are not necessarily believers, and not all theatre people attend synagogues, mosques, churches or temples. What is being described here is an experience of self-opening which is understood to be a gift to the self rather than merely one of its products; and which is expressed by those who receive it in the shape of a human gesture – a gesture expressive of total personal commitment. At this level theatre and religious ritual turn out to have a great deal in common. Within the "safe space" of a work of art, we are encouraged to take the risk of exposing our own vulnerability and frailty. Plays and corporate rituals involve a dual awareness of danger and safety; they allow us to show ourselves in spite of our self-protective urge to remain safely in hiding, strengthening us in the action of looking beyond ourselves.

This is the experience which Aristotle identified as catharsis, the very heart of the theatrical event. The kind of theatre he was describing certainly has a close affinity with religious ritual, and the phenomenon of catharsis – the word means 'purging' – takes place in both settings. Indeed, it occurs whenever danger and safety are present at the same time. Theatre and ritual are safe in the sense that they are put together in advance, so that at least the possibility of self-disclosure is expected; arrangements have been made for it. Both explicitly in religious ritual, and implicitly in theatre, we are summoned into the presence of a reality which is ostensibly terrifying to us as persons by the promise of spiritual fulfilment. In both theatre and ritual deliverance from fear comes as an experience of emotional liberation – a sense of being purged by responding in relationship to what is not ourselves. Aristotle explains how this comes about as a result of our willingness to become involved at the deepest, most personal level with someone else's sufferings; it is a deliverance brought about by the contact between fear for ourselves and pity for someone else – someone who might very well have been us . . . (*Poetics*, VI, 2, Butcher, 1951).

In catharsis we achieve distance from ourselves, our own anxieties and fears, both conscious and unconscious, by taking someone else's place in a gesture of willing identification with them. We do not do this in order to deny the reality of someone else's agony, but to comfort and strengthen them with the gift of our own loving concern. The psychotherapist Thomas Scheff describes how a mother's response to her child's anguish helps make the pain bearable by endorsing its reality and granting the child permission to weep; being allowed to cry, says Scheff, helps children bear the burdens which are "An inescapable feature of infancy as a result of intense and incommunicable feelings of separation and loss" (1979: 62). These words take on a particular resonance in the context of Christian worship!

In the relationship between self and other, the catharsis permitted by art – either theatrical or liturgical – plays a crucial role, what Donald Winnicott called a "transitional object". This is something comfortingly familiar which nevertheless has the power to transport us into an altogether unfamiliar world, a new way of relating to one another and to ourselves. Transitional objects are remarkable for their ordinariness and strangeness, commonplace reality and transcendent significance. They occupy a unique position in our awareness as symbols of betweenness: "The separation that is not a separation but a form of union" (1971: 115). Winnicott was a psychoanalyst, concerned with the inner working of the mind; but he is careful to point out that the reality he is describing here transcends the inner/outer division, for "This area of playing is not inner psyche, far from it, its existence can be seen in the things we use in order to relate to the world we share – things like art, science, politics and organized religion" (1971: 115).

Two places in which it is clearly seen at work are theatre and corporate ritual, both of which psychologically speaking, function as transitional objects. Theatre possesses a striking ability to restore us to ourselves and one another by making the reconciling action safe enough for vulnerable people to take part in. At its most fundamental level it is a way of permitting encounter by manipulating or adjusting distance, using the recognisable and familiar to put us in touch with what is radically qualitatively, dramatically, other, in a relationship of 'polar unity' (Buber's phrase) which is authentically spiritual. The same thing is demonstrably true about liturgy, as by its action we are restored to ourselves, to one another, and to God.

To summarise what has been said in this chapter about the relationship between liturgy and drama as these two human activities are embodied in theatre and corporate worship:

- Theatre and liturgy involve our ability to live imaginatively 'in two worlds' at the same time. Audiences and actors do so as a practical proposition, something they have agreed to do together; linguists and literary critics talk of metaphor and symbol, and religions of theophany and sacrament, all of which are ways of overcoming the contradiction on which theatre and worship depend.
- Theatre is 'safe' (*i.e.* 'only a play'), yet it leads into a surrender of defensiveness. This is because, like religious ritual it is an acted symbol, participating in the reality to which it is pointing.
- Theatre is a way of focusing attention and expectation upon the enactment of a story which we participate in – or emotionally inhabit – as homologous to our own; so does liturgy.
- Theatre provides the emotional distance we need to reach out beyond ourselves in order to enter into relationship with someone else and so participate in their story. This is pre-eminently the function of corporate worship.

Theatre's connection with liturgy thus concerns the very heart of our experience of drama – the way we feel drawn beyond the limiting circumstances we usually find ourselves in to engage a spiritual reality which enables us to share and lose ourselves in sharing. This is not to say that theatre always does this, of course; only that as a medium it is capable of doing it, and that when it fails to do it, it is no longer carrying out its primary purpose, that of involving personal encounter.

But this is also true of corporate worship. Those who put services together with the aim of achieving a dramatic effect, 'using drama' in order to make worship more exciting (and thus draw larger congregations) often seem to have missed the point; they concentrate on the least important aspect of theatre, its ability to create

spectacles which amuse and titillate. We may be impressed by liturgical showmanship but we are rarely convinced by it. 'Circus
theatre' and 'all-singing-all-dancing' worship are never convincingly theatrical – you must go deeper into the heart of the story to
do that. On the other hand, attempts at *trompe l'oeil* are more suspect
when they almost succeed instead of when we can easily see through
them. Theatre is never merely a trick and nor should liturgy be.

Liturgy must penetrate beyond show to something more fundamental, more essential, than this. Historians of theatre see it as
having evolved from the ritual celebration of death and rebirth
which is believed to have been associated with the end of winter and
the onset of spring. There are various accounts – conjectural of
course – of how this way of acknowledging the spiritual significance
of human experience by envisaging it as taking place within an over-
arching cosmic setting became associated with historical accounts
of heroic deeds carried out by individuals or groups of people on
behalf of the entire community. Scholars are fascinated by the
notion of a slowly developing ability to make sense of mystery by
tying it into traditions concerning actual events, which themselves
took place over centuries, or even millennia, to emerge first as ritual,
then as theatre. Dorothy Langley describes the process like this:

> The progression from ritual to theatre was probably slow and is epit-
> omised by the evolution of Greek theatre which ultimately
> developed from the worship of the god Dionysus and, or hymn that
> was sing around his altar (Hartnell, 1985: 8). This was a corporate
> event, with a chorus of fifty members who told or enacted the story
> . . . until, it is popularly believed, one actor, Thespis, slipped out
> from the chorus to enact an individual character, ending the long
> tradition and making way for solo actors to take the stage. (2006: 4)

Certainly this sheds light on the history of theatre, but it ignores
the heart of ritual, which is and always has been the spirit of worship
in the life-experience of men and women which longs for personal
meetings with the source of its personhood. For worshippers,
awareness of God's presence is an immediate reality which includes
historical events by transcending them; and worshippers are
convinced that this has always been the way. In other words, they

are unlikely to be satisfied with historical accounts of the connection between worship and drama; indeed they may prefer not to think of worship and liturgy in the context of something they are used to dismissing as simply a source of entertainment.

By talking about drama we run the risk of alarming those who are quite sure of the fact that, whatever else they may be, they are most certainly not actors. The idea of going on stage, performing before other people, terrifies me, they say; and of course they really mean it. Even professional actors can be overcome by panic when the time draws near for making their entrance. Liturgy is not like this, however. Liturgies are performed *with* other people, *for* God. The dramatic element is that of shared imagination, as all those taking part move together into a deeper understanding, a more transforming experience, of the beckoning presence of what it is that lies *beyond* imagination. When it comes to dealing with life's realities, drama definitely has its uses, and liturgy is one of these; from a religious point of view the most important one.

Aside from this, the drama which is liturgy is mercifully free from some of the most frightening aspects of theatrical performance. There are no lines to be learned – so no danger of forgetting them – and there is usually no need for rehearsal. There is no-one to criticise your performance or compare it with anyone else's. You are all in this drama together, helping one another do the best you can to make it as expressive as possible of the purpose you all share – that of praising God in the language he has chosen to inhabit, human life-experience. Here 'best' means most sincere, whole-hearted, honest – certainly not most technically accomplished or even most talented. And yet, all the same it is still drama, the acted story of our lives, human truth unfolding along with the passage of time.

From whatever angle we choose to look at it, liturgy is deeply personal. Throughout the world, in all kinds of society, personal identity is enriched by the acted symbolism of corporate rites of passage. Is it our spiritual life, our psychological health, our group awareness and social commitment that is fed by our involvement in them? Obviously it is all three of these aspects of our common human experience, because it is all of our self that we bring along to be transformed. Nothing is lost of our individuality, while our belonging together is confirmed in the sharing. If we claim owner-ship of our liturgies in the way described here, taking hold of the medium and using it to communicate in the way that, in word and sacrament, God reveals himself to us, we allow ourselves to respond to an initiative which is never simply human, because it summons us to reach out in our own life-stories to the eternal Story of Life.

To be connected with others in the liturgy is to be renewed in our individual identity – a spiritual truth which appears to be a psychological paradox. The fact is, however, that we learn to tol-erate our aloneness through our relationship with others; to tolerate it and also to value its power to turn us toward others. Liturgy illustrates this more vividly than any human activity; more vividly in fact than drama, because its purpose in revealing truth about human life is plainly stated as response to the invitation to 'draw near'. The use of narrative is the same, but here the story is the one told us by God.

Our faith as Christians is story-based; the Holy Spirit addresses us through our personal stories by the way he has involved us in his own. The liturgies sketched here are offered as ways of helping us to understand how we ourselves may contribute to the living out of divine history by learning how to embrace our own experience so that it is genuinely our own, for only thus can one value it as he intends us to do, as our own part of his eternal purpose. The message of liturgy is simply this: that the having is in the sharing.

Liturgy, then, is a story in which, through Christ, we ourselves are the narrators; a drama in which we are all actors. This is a simple enough idea, not hard to grasp but so often forgotten, as we allow ourselves to withdraw our attention from what it is we are actually doing when we join in worship; what it is we are really committing ourselves to in the action of reaffirming our faith in this way. It is so very easy to half-do something which involves so much more than simply fitting in with what everyone else is doing. Nowadays, when our churches are often not as crowded as they once were, the signif-icance we ourselves give to the action of sharing liturgy (or the absence of any intention of so doing) stands out more clearly than ever before.

Working at liturgy in the way suggested here helps us to realise how, by learning to engage with our own stories – embracing them and making them our own so that we are used to living in them – we contribute to the living out of the divine story which we all share together. Thus, by sharing the liturgical story we help our own to grow in depth of meaning and strength of corporate witness. The developmental aspect of liturgy is thrown into high relief by this level of participation. By taking account of the actual things which have happened to us and making the effort to see them in the wider context of a life lived in and through relationship with other people, we learn to give them a value they would not possess as isolated incidents, separate happenings lacking the power to affect the overall significance of our life; interesting as individual experiences, but not as human testimony. For Christians, as for genuinely religious people of any kind whatever, such an attitude to life is impossible. Along with those who have studied human psychological development in depth and in accordance with their findings, we are bound to conclude that we really cannot look at life in such a way and remain fully alive, fully human, because this involves taking responsibility for the way our ability to live in relationship develops by becoming more not less concerned with the meaning which emerges from the way our lives 'hang together'. Psychologists tell us that personal relationship involves being simultaneously connected with others and separate from them. I can find no more powerful validation of this truth than that provided by a Christian's experience of sharing in the pilgrimage which is our liturgy, in which, for everyone who allows themselves to be personally involved, the medium itself is the transforming message.

As with plays, so with church services: the drama comes to life in doing the message, not just thinking about it – however inspiring this may be – and in doing it all together. Liturgy lives wherever thought and feelings are allowed to become *showing forth*. It is the fully personal expression of the most personal of all relationships. Here is a 'wordless liturgy', so called by those who put it together after an afternoon of exploring how ideas and feelings of the most personal kind may be shared within a space specially set aside for this kind of self-expression:

Love Feast

A

- Say hello to one another in an informal way (shaking hands, embracing or simply smiling, according to taste).
- Walk anywhere in the space available at your own speed. After a minute or two, start to move outwards until you are at the edges of the space, where you can either remain standing or sit down. The leader announces a time of prayer.
- You may pray silently or aloud, about yourself, one another and the world.
- The leader sums the prayers up and announces that people are invited to join in a symbolic action of sharing together – a Love Feast.
- The leader invites someone to read an account of the Last Supper from the New Testament, after which a psalm of thanksgiving is said or sung.
- There is a time of silence.

B

- After a few moments the leader draws everyone into the centre of the room to sit down together in a circle around a loaf of bread and a flask of wine.
- Everyone sits silently, holding hands.
- The leader says something like "Let the Feast begin" or "Now it's time to start".
- A member of the group stands up and goes over to the loaf of bread and another to the flask of wine. Bread and wine are passed around the group until all present have partaken. (Silence is preserved.)

C

- The leader invites the group to pray and prayers of thanksgiving are said, either privately or aloud.
- One by one, stand up and leave the circle, after saying goodbye and exchanging blessings with everyone present.
- Form a ring outside the circle of chairs and hold hands.
- Sing a hymn or a song which people know and love.

V | Celebrating Life

This chapter takes the theme of the last one a vital step further onwards into the realm of worship and liturgy.

Liturgy and Rites of Passage

Just as a play's action hinges upon a central confrontation, a 'moment of birth' which expresses what the play is about, so religious rituals revolve around the contradiction between humans and divine; a confrontation which once engaged carries with it a promise of deliverance. The shape of spiritual inclinations conforms to the scenario we have been considering – the story of human transformation-through-displacement and disintegration which leaves room for 'newness of life'.

Arnold van Gennep, a Dutch anthropologist, drew attention to a pattern of corporate 'rituals of passage' which has been taken as the prototype for understanding initiation ceremonies throughout the world. Van Gennep (1960) drew attention to the part played in the way the indigenous Australian peoples whom he studied celebrated important occasions which occurred in the lives of communities and their individual members by what he distinguished as "preliminal, terminal and post terminal rites", the first being "rites of separation from a previous world" and the last "ceremonies of incorporation into a new world". In between, however, are what he describes as "liminal rites, sometimes called threshold rituals". Rites of passage, says Van Gennep, are always triadic, even though we may prefer to think of them in simple terms as 'before' and 'after', thereby avoiding having to contemplate, and live through, the psychological difficulty involved in crossing the actual threshold and finding ourselves in a place which is 'neither here nor there'. In this of course they resemble stories and plays. They are also necessary for a shared sense of purpose in human life because they give shape, and consequently meaning, to belonging as a person among people.

The importance of such rituals has long been neglected in Western culture, as indeed have the rituals themselves, except within specifically religious settings; but their importance remains and is likely to do so, wherever people meet to celebrate important stages in the lives of individuals and groups of people. Erik Erikson, the developmental psychologist, speaks of

> A certain kind of informal and yet prescribed interplay between persons who repeat it at meaningful intervals and in recurring contexts. While such interplay may not mean much more (at least to the participants) than 'this is the way we do things', it has, we claim, an adaptive value for all participants and for their group living. For it furthers and guides from the beginning of existence, that stage-wise instinctual process that must do for human adaptation what the instinctive fit into a section of nature will do for an animal species. (1985, vol. 3)

"This first achievement of human identity as 'ritualisation'," Erikson says, "supports the joint need . . . for a mutuality of recognition" (p. 44). In fact it does so by embodying a community's relationship with an overarching source of meaning, a "mutuality of recognition" acknowledged as being particularly important and necessary at times involving or necessitating changes in the way human beings regard themselves, one another and the world they live in.

Ven Gennep's 'rites of passage' recognise the achievement of vital change within an individual's life as a person in relationship with her or his fellow women and men by solemnly 'homologising' it with the changing seasons of the year. The passage rituals take place in groups of three ceremonies because of the special significance three-ness has in human living and dying because it stands for the way in which we approach experiences which we recognise as *important* and *new*; things which challenge our ability to cope with life in the way we have done before. It is not as easy as we may think it should be for us to move into a new relationship with the realities of living and dying simply by deciding to cross the line which our minds draw so effortlessly between ideas of past and future. For the new way of being which we contemplate to be really itself, really new, the old one must have been laid to rest in some recognizable and memorable way. As we saw, drama is always the way really important things are communicated; because it is the way space is created 'round' whatever it is that needs to be specially highlighted and brought home. It is in fact a reciprocal action. The importance of the event makes it dramatic and the dramatic way it is presented underlines its importance. Taken together they signify something new, a break with the past. In the stories we tell about ourselves we lead up to and then away from the central event which is the main point of the narrative:

- a *beginning*, when we turn our attention to the task in hand and prepare ourselves for something whose actuality we have not yet experienced;
- a *middle*, when despite all our efforts at assimilation-by-anticipation, we are suddenly in 'over our heads' so that we 'don't know which way to turn'; and
- an *end*, when we look back at where we have been, and at the effort it has taken us to arrive where we are, and what was once so terrifyingly new is now well on the way to being reassuringly old.

The main point, then, is the incursion of a genuinely new state of affairs. This is the shape of all real changes – ones which are not simply adjustments or modifications. Three is the number of clarity and 'definition' and a threefold progression is needed to bring home the over-riding significance of the statements we make. This is true of humour as well as solemnity; no catchphrase seems as funny as it does the third time of hearing.

The year's story and the story of someone's achievement of adult status within the community are told together, and the telling is threefold, to express its importance and underline its transformative reality. In this way an event in someone's life is sanctified by identification with perfection – three, the perfect number, as Pythagoras called it, because in the most striking way, as beginning, middle and end, it signifies a complete action. The theological meaning of threeness has often been noted, not only in Christian theology and liturgy but elsewhere. Any initiatory ritual in any religious tradition is likely to adopt the rite of passage because of its eloquence as the sign of initiation into wholeness. In this way its meaning is inalienably religious and any ceremony which has been arranged so that the principal events follow the same pattern implies this search for completeness, the intention to aspire beyond past, or current limitations and so enter new territory, and share in a new way of being. This is the truth of Mircea Eliadé's dictum that "Initiation and its patterns [are] understandably linked with the very structure of spiritual life" (1965: 119). Certainly every act of worship is, in this sense, an initiation.

In the next part of this chapter we shall look at ways in which these 'worship-initiations' may be put together so that the message is transmitted by, or embodied in, the result is that their shape stands clearly out. The following are not intended as finished acts of worship, but only as workshops. First of all we consider the initiatory ritual most celebrated by anthropologists and historians of religion – a puberty rite.

A Ceremony to Mark Someone's Coming of Age (basic form)

Part One (Preliminary)

1   Ceremonial entry of congregation who process into the worship area. This may be done with musical accompaniment, but is probably better in silence.
2   Ceremonial entry of the person to be established as an adult member of the worshipping community. He or she takes up a position detached from the rest.
3   A master of ceremonies announces the purpose of the occasion, namely, the congregation's intention to receive this person as a new member of their community, sharing in its identity as a body of people who themselves are in a special,

privileged relationship with one another and the Truth which sustains this. In the passage of a new member, they proclaim and establish their own passage. This is done in song and movement.

Part Two (Liminal)

This is the time dedicated to the candidate's spiritual identification with the source of new life, and may be portrayed as a baptism or a symbolic birth. We are reminded in no uncertain terms that "No one can see the kingdom of God without being born from above". Nicodemus, in St John's Gospel, speaks of "entering a second time into the mother's womb", commenting on the total absurdity of such an idea; he is right, of course. This is not something human beings can do of their own ability. This part of the transformation ritual belongs solely to God. To extend Nicodemus' image, this is where our personal story is taken up by a completely new one. We are born into someone else's story, given the Spirit of Someone Else. This is not something we do ourselves, but this is the place in our humanly constructed ritual which we dedicate to it. In this part of the rite we embrace our transformation by identifying with a story which was not our own. This may be expressed symbolically in as many ways as we may be inspired to embody it. As it is a story about change which is salutary and radical, its imagery will centre upon hardship endured and progress interrupted or prevented, as the central figure within the rite's symbolism is faced with a situation from which, in human terms, there seems to be no escape.

Part Three (Post-Liminal)

In this final part the community of worshippers proclaim their participation in the victorious story about participation in the rite, along with their new member they embrace the deliverance described by the man who was born blind and has his sight given him – not simply restored but given, bestowed as release from darkness into light:

"The man called Jesus made mud, spread it on my eyes and said to me, 'Go to Siloam and wash.' Then I went and washed and received my sight." (John 9: 11)

The significance of the Fourth Gospel for Christian liturgy is well accredited:* I am calling on it here as a paradigm for the final stage in every individual initiation ritual. The old state of affairs is over, the new one is now here. The congregation rejoices as one person over the renewal of one of its members.

A Liturgy for Renewing the Story of a Community

If individuals possess stories, then so do communities. With regard to meanings which are shared by groups who worship together, James Hopewell (1987) clearly demonstrated that church congregations can only be understood on the basis of the stories members tell of themselves and their communities as they struggle to preserve the corporate identity which represents their own particular history.

"We are the people who have stayed together in good times and in bad ones, and the knowledge of the events we have survived together makes us who we are . . . " The corporate mythology of congregations is particularly tough and resistant to change. It is just as deeply entrenched in its consciousness as the personal narrative of its individual members; in fact it is impossible to disentangle the 'separate' story from the 'corporate' one.

At this level it would be better to speak of refreshing a story rather than renewing it, although spiritually (and psychologically) speaking the two are actually indistinguishable from each other. In the liturgy we shall be considering here a congregation that refreshes itself at the source of its shared story, which is one already understood in terms of an over-arching transcendent narrative in and through which the distinction between individual and corporate has ceased to have any real, spiritual, meaning at all. The transformative power of this ritual is experienced by those taking part as a sharing signifying belonging which is already attained but which, because of the human nature of those taking part, requires refreshment and remembrance:

Do this in memory of me . . .

* Cf. Cullman (1953).

Part One (Pre-Liminal)

The congregation is led into a ceremony in which it represents the terms of its belonging together, the identity which it is conscious of sharing and intends to celebrate. During this time it calls to mind its chronic spiritual frailty, and the personal and social responsibility it takes for the results of this frailty; but then it reminds itself of another identity it shares, one re-created by participation in a transformed and transformative Story. During this part of the liturgy texts are sung and danced as well as read and preached; and some of the messages are communicated gesturally in ways that are spontaneous and immediate.

Part Two (Liminal)

In this part of the liturgy the terms of the congregation's transformed story are acted out in a way which calls for deep personal involvement, presenting as it does the cost required of the story's hero – with whom the congregation as a body and its individual members are spiritually identified, and to whom they now come for reinforcement of their own participation in the agony and the triumph of his story. To quote again from the fourth Gospel, "Let anyone who is thirsty come to me" (John 7: 37). Again this section may be embodied in any number of ways – although it would be hard to imagine a more vivid expression than the 'painful meal' around which the Christian Eucharist takes place.

Part Three (Post Liminal)

Those who share this 'new story' inhabit a world whose values have been reversed, not simply modified or improved ("Lord, are you going to wash my feet?"). This last part of the 'Liturgy of Refreshment' celebrates the experience of new life which is personal and shared; personal *because* shared, in which love is freely given and received. Congregations re-discover their unique identity in the action of surrendering it to a wider belonging. This is very much a home-coming ceremony, both in terms of being an image of disuse for the rite as a completed gesture, and of the theology presented here in ritual form, which is a message about the fulfilment of God's purpose, the closure of his story. It is this knowledge which confirms the congregation in its belonging, however painful in terms of inci-

dental set backs and unforeseen disasters that may continue to be –
this truth which refreshes for the journey.

These two passage rituals are very different in detail, while
preserving an identical outline. Both make use of a variety of ways
of proclaiming a story, the most striking of all being that they themselves are story-shaped. This story is one about discovering and
nurturing a relationship with the source of life; its content is explicitly religious. At the same time, however, its form links it with all our
human attempts to make sense of being alive, and every serious
effort we make to behave in ways which are authentically human
and personal.

As Mary and Kenneth Gergen put it:

> We understand our lives as a story, history as a story, the cosmos as
> a story. In effect, the story form structures our understandings and
> our actions. (2003: 61)

In corporate rites of passage God is known as the Storyteller who
authenticates our storytelling by identifying it as his own.

Some Christian Passage Rites

A: Baptism

The history of Christian baptism bears witness to its nature as a
threefold complex of ceremonies. Initiation took place in the first
Christian centuries according to a well-defined succession of pre-
liminal, liminal and post liminal rites. The evidence provided by the
New Testament itself suggests that initiation constituted three
stages: preparation, dipping into water with repetition of the name
of Jesus or the Holy Trinity, and laying on of hands or anointing. In
the third century AD, Hippolytus and Tertullian indicate a pattern
which elaborates on this, beginning with a series of preliminal
actions (instruction of catechumens, blessing of the water, and
candidates' threefold renunciation of the devil), leading into the
baptism itself – a threefold affirmation accompanying a triple
immersion – culminatin in the post-liminal phase of anointing,
laying on of hands by the bishop with prayers for the descent of Holy

Spirit and the signing of the cross, and a symbolic 'first meal' of honey and milk for those who were newly born in Christ (Noakes, 1979: 91*f*).

The liturgical order persists during succeeding centuries, even after the growth of infant baptism has made it impracticable in its original detail. The modified order consisted of:

The Pre-liminal actions:
- admission of the catechumens.
- enrolment and preparation of the candidates.
- a ceremony in which the candidates' ears and nostrils are symbolically anointed and Mark 7: 34 read in Latin and Aramaic ('*Effala*, that is, be opened'). Candidates are then stripped and anointed as a way of exorcising them prior to baptism. They renounce the devil and agree to follow Christ.
- Holy Spirit is invoked (*Epiclesis*) in the blessing of the waters, and the sign of the cross made over them.

The Liminal Rite
- candidates are immersed.
- their heads are anointed.
- their feet are ceremonially washed.

The Post-Liminal Rite
- candidates are dressed in white garments.
- they perform actions (involving blessing, laying on of hands and anointing, exchanging the kiss of peace) symbolising the Church's acceptance of these new Christians and the continuity of Holy Spirit's work.
- the neophytes, dressed in white and carrying candles, process into church.

It is fascinating to see how the threefold pattern is preserved in modern liturgies. The 'Rite of Baptism for Children', produced in 1969 by the International Committee on English in the Liturgy, has five sections (Reception of the Child; Celebration of God's Word; Prayer of Exorcism and Anointing before Baptism; Celebration of the Sacrament; Conclusion of the Rite). The first three fall naturally into the shape of a pre-liminal rite of *preparation* and *separation*: first of all, reception involving the signing of the Cross and parents' and godparents' declaration of their responsibilities; instruction in the meaning and significance of what is to follow, in the form of gospel readings and a short homily; symbolic actions of exorcism and anointing preparing the child itself for its journey. Then, in the rite's central section the child is baptised, parents and godparents responding in the person of someone who is too young to speak up for him – or herself. The child's new state of being is symbolised by the imagery of anointing with the 'chrism of salvation', to show that she or he is now 'in Christ', a fact expressed by the action of clothing and the reception of a lighted candle by one of his or her proxies. So ends the crucial liminal phase. The post-liminal movement now follows in the form of a hymn and procession, and prayers of thanksgiving. The Celebrant sums up with a Blessing which rehearses the significance of everything which has just been taking place. The Anglican 'Holy Baptism' service in *Common Worship* (2000) falls into four main sections; 'Preparation', 'Liturgy of the Word', 'Liturgy of Baptism', 'Sending Out'. However, as with the 1969 order, the opening rite involves more than one division here. Preparation and Liturgy of the Word belong together as a 'rite of separation' in which candidates are prepared for their journey through the water of rebirth. (The arrangement here reproduces the traditional form of Eucharistic worship, in which 'The Liturgy of the Word' represents the pre-liminal section, and the sacramental action itself is included as 'The Liturgy of the Sacrament.) In all these baptismal services the two outer movements are more 'public' than the inner one contained by them, beginning as they do with a corporate declaration of intent, and ending with a united celebration of the new state of affairs brought about by God's action within the rite .

B: Marriage

Christian marriage also was originally a threefold succession of rites (or of ritual stages), the liminal phase corresponding to the special 'protected' interval between betrothal and nuptial ceremonies (Davies 1972). The betrothal ceremony itself was tripartite, consisting of:

- the giving of a financial pledge that the marriage will eventually take place.
- the bestowal of ring and veil, signifying the future wife's change of status and her undertaking of household responsibilities as wielder of exclusive jurisdiction over hearth and home.
- the kiss and joining of hands, to seal the bond.

All this, along with the liminal period between betrothal and the wedding itself – which was also a three-part ceremony – is now contained within a single rite, the unambiguous meaning of which is brought home by its shape:

- *The preliminal phase* of separation, in which the precise purpose of the rite is distinguished from action of other kinds:
  1 the meaning of Christian marriage, illustrated from the bible.
  2 the public announcement of this couple's intention to marry and their own declaration (shared by the congregation in Common Worship) that they know no lawful impediment for the wedding.
  3 prayer, scripture reading and sermon, all of which set the scene for marriage.

(In *Common Worship* these constitute the 'Introduction' section of the rite, divided into five parts; in 'The Rite of Marriage for use in the Dioceses of England and Wales', however, they are divided as here, into three sections: 'Entrance Rite', 'Liturgy of the Word' and 'Consent'.)

- *The Liminal Phase* or 'crossing of the threshold' in which
  1 the couple make their promises to each other.
  2 a ring is given or rings are exchanged.
  3 the priest or minister proclaims that God has now joined the couple in an inseparable way.

(The intimacy of this part of the service is stressed by the blessing of the ring, which is held in place by each partner during their exchange of vows, and the symbolic binding together of the "couples'" clasped hands.)

- *The Post-liminal phase* , in which
  1 the marriage is blessed.
  2 the legal requirements are carried out, thus establishing the extra liturgical validity of the contract.
  3 prayers are said for the couple's future life together and the congregation is dismissed with a blessing.

(Husband and wife lead the procession out, members of the wedding party following two-by-two, the bride's and groom's families walking together to demonstrate the new united family.)

C: Funerals

The original extended rite gave those concerned more time to come to terms with a major life change. Sometimes we may find that the things which happen to us require more time set aside specifically for the purpose of working through a painful process of change; sometimes even the rites we have are inadequate in their ability to symbolise their ancient meaning. The most obvious example is the funeral ritual. Among Protestant Christians the funeral has lost its central and final movements; and it is this truncated liturgy which provides the only ceremony available for the great majority of people who do not belong to any church at all. The final rite of reintegration has been lost, departing with the universal practice of remembering the dead each year at the feasts of All Saints and All Souls, and with it has gone the permission to stop grieving which was its psychological purpose, marking as it did the end of a liminal 'space for grief' after the rite, or progression of ceremonies which constituted the preliminal phase – now in many cases, the only one which remains. The liminal movement of the extended rite was rich in imagery providing an analogue of the state of mind and soul of people who find themselves caught up in emotional turmoil, thus homologising human experience with an over-arching divine intention. Modern church practice tends to lack ways of dealing with this sort of unfinished business (Grainger 1988a & b, 1998). Publicly we keep our grief private and hope that we can somehow manage to forget. We need not signal its end because we never, officially, ever had it. It is in this vital area of life, perhaps more than any other, that we need adequate rites of passage.

We can learn from this that merely having rituals is not enough; we need to know more about the way they function, and why they are so fundamental to our well-being. We need to value them as an irreplaceable source of our self understanding, untranslatable into any other idiom, communicating truths requiring our personal and social attention. We need to rediscover what we have come to take for granted, the liturgical heritage which we already possess, and to have the courage to experiment in ways of deepening our own involvement in it.

Liturgy and Unfinished Business

Rites of passage are concerned with the relationship between the old and the new. They take place at the frontier between life and death, and their purpose is to usher us across this into a new kind of life, another kind of newness. Hence their association in people's minds with death and dying. In cultures throughout the world the most important passage rite is undoubtedly the funeral service. Unless people have had a funeral they are not deemed to be properly dead; if they have not properly died they remain ineligible for any future life. Death, as Hamlet puts it, is "the country from which no traveller returns"; its sole port of entry is the funeral. Everyone must pass through this gate. There is no going round it, if you are a human being. From this point of view, to die is the mark of being human.

Hubert McCabe describes Hell as being populated by those "confronted by God but unable to die into him" (1964: 21). Ghost cultures throughout the world regard the funeral as the means of keeping the dead in the dimension of being to which they belong; in other words, preserving their humanity beyond the grave. Otherwise they have nowhere to go and nothing to be. The world of the established and socially incorporated dead – those whose reality has been properly preserved by the action of the living – is understood as impinging on the world of their successors, in some cases actually overlapping it. At certain times of the year they are ritually welcomed back into the fellowship of the living so that the presence of the dead may become an essential part of the corporate life of society. In this way the past is used to reinforce the present and give courage for the future (Grainger 1988a).

This may seem to us to be so far from our own attitude to life and death (and particularly ghosts) that it is almost unintelligible. In fact it is much nearer to our own way of thinking than it may seem to be at first. We, too, are eager to "keep the dead in their place". It is important to understand that these attitudes of mind towards death are implicit within our own culture. Life and death objectified as separate territories, with a gateway set in its own special position "between", correspond to personal experiences within the lives of individuals and communities even in the most secularised, postmodern societies – wherever, in fact, funerals continue to be asked for and appropriate rites of passage carried out.

Certainly, the trauma of bereavement can bring with it experiences of unfinished business which are very like this. Our minds are invaded by the living presence of someone who we know is dead. The knowledge that such 'haunting' is irrational makes us all the more determined to ignore it, deny it, repress it, and if we are successful it becomes even more oppressive as it emerges in the form of symptoms of emotional disturbance. As we strive to dissociate ourselves from it, so it becomes stronger and more oppressive. "This is nothing to do with me," we say; "I disclaim all responsibility for it. It has no business here with me. It is a ghost." And so it is. Somehow the gate between the two worlds has been left open. The funeral rite of passage exists for those who find themselves afflicted like this.

Funerals, then, are archetypal passage rituals. It seems very likely indeed that they are the oldest corporate rituals of all. Life holds innumerable 'deaths and entrances' which are no less real for being less literal; in fact they draw their reality from their participation in the literal fact of death. They are reminders of mortality, and as such they benefit from liturgical recognition. Like ghosts, they need to be *realised* in order to be dealt with appropriately. The seemingly irrational behaviour of some bereaved people bears witness to the fact – the scrupulous setting of a customary place, the nightdress always arranged lovingly on the empty pillow, the chair reverently set for the master of the house. Although these things and others like them are easily dismissed as evidence of a naïve belief in the literal presence of the dead, they are evidence of another kind of human reality – that of people's ability to assert their own personal meaning in situations which make practical action of any kind absurdly impractical; the realism of gestures which, even when they are not the sign of actual religious belief in an afterlife, are all the same assertions of the reality of human experience. It is this kind of significant human action which helps preserve sanity against the threat of disintegration; when, because of the loss of a vital member, our personal universe is in danger of falling apart, taking all sense of reality and purpose with it, gestures of this kind hold us together by reinforcing our sense of being real in a world which has substance.

These solitary gestures are focused passage rites, the best we can manage in the solitude of grief, yet powerful all the same. Rituals and rites of passage, says Robert Fulghum, "often take place where words cannot go – in a solitary, secret inner kingdom where just knowing is enough . . . they anchor us to a centre while freeing us to move on and confront the everlasting unpredictability of life." This, he says, is because "structure gives us a sense of security. And that sense of security is the ground of meaning" (1995: 244, 261).

Even for agnostic people, then, rites point beyond, as 'metaphors of a larger design'. In the next section we shall give an example of liturgy used as a way of dealing with the unfinished business of making sense of life.

A

Simon is a member of a church discussion group which meets on a weekly basis during most of the year. He is a post-graduate student at a local university. A highly intelligent young man of 30, he has spent the last ten years working in disadvantaged parts of the world, and this combination of academic ability and experience 'in the field' tends to make some other members of the group feel uncomfortable: "It's as if you have to keep on your feet all the time, in case you say something stupid." Simon himself is very conscious of the effect he has on the group, and having made his views known early on in the session, tends to spend the remainder of the evening in silence.

Tonight he has had no chance to do this because the group have taken it in turns to describe their own personal view of themselves. ("Say what sort of person you think you are. Try to do it in a couple of sentences if you can.") When it came to Simon's turn to do this, he simply said he couldn't do it; he had no idea what sort of person he was.

Angela:	What do you mean?
Simon:	What I said. I've no idea what I'm like.
Philip:	Well, then, who do you take after? Everybody takes after someone. I think with me it's my mother.
Simon:	I don't take after anyone, certainly not my mother, who's a wonderful person.
Angela:	Well, your father then. Do you take after your father?

Simon doesn't say anything. After a pause, another member of the group asks him what his father was like. Speaking in a slow, calm, reserved voice, he tells them . . .

It turns out that Simon's father was a senior RAF officer – so senior that his family scarcely ever saw him for more than a few days at a time. Simon admired him a great deal and tried his best to be as much like him as he could be, which was hard because he never really knew what his father was actually like. In Simon's own phrase, there was "a kind of father-shaped gap" in his childhood. Simon received the upbringing considered appropriate for the son of an officer and gentleman – boarding school and Cambridge college – before going on to theological college (not quite so acceptable, perhaps) and an opportunity to follow his own choice of career.

Then suddenly the Air Commodore died, at the height of his own career and without the chance of either getting to know the other. Simon described how he felt when this happened; the efforts he made to gather every memento of the dead man he could possibly lay his hands on, trying to piece together some sort of presence of his father, someone identifiable, someone to identify *with*. "I never had the chance to talk to him and tell him I loved him, you see; he was just a memory of someone who would be angry if I didn't hold my knife and fork properly."

The result seems to have been to leave Simon knowing how to behave but not how to be, an oversight he attempted to make up for by criticising other people's behaviour, which he did without fear or favour, "like the cheeky bastard I am".

Someone asked him if he had been able to attend his father's funeral. He said he hadn't, that his mother didn't think it was appropriate; he was in the middle of his ordination examinations, "and your father wouldn't have thought it necessary".

Philip:	What a pity that was.
Simon:	Yes it was. I might have had an opportunity to say goodbye which would've been something.
Mary (who hasn't spoken yet):	*Hello* and goodbye.

Together the group decided to set about working together to give Simon's father a firmer outline in his son's awareness so that they could construct a special 'memorial liturgy' for this unique purpose; to give Simon a stronger sense of whom he was *himself*. This mainly consisted of playing games together in which they exchanged letters with people out of their own life stories who they were longing to hear from and to whom they had some things vitally important to say; later on the letters 'became' the people themselves as individual dramas were improvised and the workshop began to move into another phase. With a great deal of support and encouragement, Simon allowed the story of his relationship with his father to be acted out by the two members of the group he trusted most (Philip and Mary), at first simply watching in silence, then taking over as director, telling them what to say and how to say it. Although this was played as a drama it was not, in the usual sense of the word, *dramatic*. In fact the whole episode wads tentative and low key out of respect for Simon's feelings. Simon, however, was moved more than offended by having his feelings made public in this way; as time went on he took more and more part in the drama, so that by the end it was Simon himself who 'made the running', the rest of the group joining in to give him support. It was later on, during the

Memorial Liturgy for Simon's Father, celebrated in church later the same week, that his control gave way and against all his principles (and those of his father), Simon wept.

A Memorial Liturgy for Simon's Father

(The Minister on this occasion was Angela.)

Part I. Everybody sang a hymn, one associated with the RAF.

The Minister welcomed the congregation, first formally, 'In the name of Christ', and then more personally, in her own words.

The Minister said a sentence from the Bible chosen to express the love which exists among members of the same family.

She went on to announce the reason for this service – that it was being held in order to remember Simon's father as an airman, certainly, but in this service mainly as a family man, as Simon's father. She went on to introduce a friend of Simon's parents, someone who knew his father in both these capacities, saying that he would be sharing some memories of him after they had listened to "what the Bible has to say about families".

One of the group (Andrew) read from St Luke's Gospel (Jesus with the Elders, Chapter 2, vv. 21-41).

After another hymn had been sung, this time one of Simon's favourites, his father's friend spoke about the dead man. He only spoke for a few minutes, concentrating on his love for his family, and particularly some of the things he remembered him saying about his son.

Now there was a pause in the service, marking the end of the first part. Music was played, ushering in **Part II**.

The Minister invited people to share prayers and memories. At this point Simon got up to say something about his father, but found himself unable to speak calmly enough to do this. So he read a poem he had written, addressed personally to the dead man.

The Minister gathered up people's prayers; "the spoken ones and the prayers of our hearts."

Everybody sang a hymn (ushering in Part III).

The Minister read a passage from the Bible giving thanks to God for his providence across the generations.

All sang Psalm 100 ('Make a joyful noise to the Lord . . . ').

The Minister announced that the purpose of the liturgy was fulfilled, and that together the congregation had accompanied Simon to a new kind of meeting with his father. "So let us now give one another a sign of peace."

The final hymn was sung and the Grace said by all present.

B

'Making a fresh start' and 'laying to rest' are the same thing. This is not as obvious as it appears to be, however, because of a human tendency to try to concentrate on one idea and ignore – or misinterpret – the other. 'Laying to rest' doesn't simply mean 'burying'. It means burying with the appropriate honours – in other words, giving what has gone before the benefit of having really existed, really happened. 'Laying to rest' is not to deny or repress or, as people seem to like saying nowadays, 'draw a line under' something (or someone). On the contrary, it is to establish something or someone as real but not present. Really belonging to the past. This is the case whatever one actually believes about the past, as to whether or not it is contactable. Christians believe that it is, as do members of other religions. It is considerably easier to think so if you believe in God; but many who say that are not in this sense believers are definite about it – they may not know where the past is, but they are definitely within reach of it, one way or another.

Sally was not a churchgoer. She only thought of herself as a Christian in a vague, undefined sense. She was in her mid-twenties, working in a bank in a London suburb and living at home with her parents and younger brother, who was still at school. Although not a regular worshipper, Sally was fond of churches, particularly empty ones. She would push the door to see if it had been left unlocked; if it had she would creep in and sit in a pew at the back and enjoy the quietness. She would only do this when she was at a safe distance from home. It wasn't something she wanted other people to know about. She didn't know anyone else who did stupid things like that . . .

This is where I found her, sitting guiltily at the back of the cathedral. She was on a visit to an old school-friend who lived here in the north of England and she had "just popped in to get a few minutes' peace". (Our cathedral is in the centre of the city.) Noticing that she looked unhappy, I hovered around pretending to be busy doing something or other just out of sight; but when Sally started to weep I moved across the aisle and sat down beside her. She looked alarmed and ashamed, as if she had been caught misbehaving – whether this was because she was weeping in church or weeping at all, or both these things, I don't know. I asked her why she was sad. There was no reply for a few moments, then "Well, I suppose I could tell *you*." Meaning, I suppose, that both I and the building were at a safe distance from any kind of come-back which could possibly affect her in any way. She was wrong about this, though.

Sally was grieving, but not for a person. She mourned the loss of the job around which she had built her life for the last five years, which can seem a very long time when you are young. In a way, of course, she *was* grieving for a person – herself; she wept for the Sally she used to be, busy and happy, feeling useful and important, the centre of a network of friends, most of whom had been fellow workers with whom she would almost certainly now lose touch. Life would never be the same. Here, in the cathedral, the truth had suddenly hit home. The future revealed itself before her, not a pathway but a chasm, a great pit of emptiness.

She said she had heard me moving about in the back of the building. What was I so busy doing? I said that I was getting ready for a wedding later in the morning, realising at the same time that mentioning other people's happiness was not really very tactful. Sally was interested, however: "When I *eventually* get married it's going to be in church," she said, "with a proper church service." I pointed out to her that you can have services celebrating other things as well as weddings.

"Like what?" she asked.

"Well, services are a good way of finishing things as well as starting them off. They celebrate what's important and needs celebrating," I said. "Like having worked five years in a bank, for instance."

Sally's Service

(I was the Minister.)

I

All: Hymn (Sally's favourite from school.)

Minister: Surely goodness and mercy shall follow me all the days of my life, and I shall dwell in the house of the Lord my whole life long. (Ps 23, v. 6)

All: Praise the Lord.

Minister: We have come here today to celebrate an achievement. Sally has finished working in ——— and is ready to move on. She will take many memories with her – some happy, some sad; times when the job made her feel angry, times when it seemed just the right job for her; times when she welcomed new colleagues, times when she had to say goodbye to people she had become fond of. Five years is a long time to stay in one job nowadays. Five years is a real achievement.

All: Hymn or song

II

Minister: Lord God our Father, we offer Sally's work at the bank to you.

All: In the name of Jesus Christ our Lord.

Minister: Sally has written down some of the things she remembers from the last five years. She's going to come up and put them on the altar table. Some of the things she's written are happy, some sad. Some were easy to write down, others not so easy. They are all going to be offered to God, just the same. (This happens.)
Sally says that there's one which she would like to share with *us*, so I've asked her to read it out.
(Sally does so and is applauded by the congregation. She returns to her seat.)

All: Hymn (On this occasion, 'When I survey the wondrous cross')

III

Minister: Please remain standing, while ———— (one of Sally's friends) reads a poem which is one of Sally's favourites. Then stay standing while I lead us in prayers.

Minister: (after the poem) Lord God our Father, we commend the rest of Sally's life to your loving care. May it be a long and happy one. Help her, we pray, to build on the achievement of the last five years as she moves on to the next stage of her journey through life. We say together the prayer Jesus taught us:

All: Our Father . . .

Minister: Glory be to the Father, and to the Son, and to the Holy Spirit.

All: As it was in the beginning, is now and shall be for ever.

All: Hymn (Processional, Sally and her friend leading.)

C

Advent is the season of the Christian year which includes the four Sundays which lead up to Christmas Day. The word itself is Latin for 'coming', and during this particular time the Church traditionally concentrates its thought upon the two 'comings' of Christ – as the world's Redeemer, a baby born in Bethlehem, and as the final Judge of Creation at the end of time. Advent Sunday itself is celebrated as the beginning of the Christian year, a time to lay the old year to rest in order to begin the drama of Christ's birth – a drama which reaches its climactic point at Christmas itself. For Christians, then, Advent is mainly significant as the festival of beginnings and endings, of saying goodbye to the old and welcoming what is new.

It is very much a time festival: the theological meaning of the events in which Christ transformed 'before' into 'after' (an *after* which is, for Christians, always *now*) is, of course, embodied in the Easter Festival. But, so far as the passage of minutes, hours and days is concerned, so far as these things are inseparable from our human experience, Advent has a special meaning. As Christians we inhabit the Christian year, laying it to rest at Advent so that we will be ready to nurture it into its new life in time for Christmas.

The following liturgy is an attempt to tackle this particular job in as explicit a way as possible. An Advent Eucharist would say it more powerfully, I realise, because only a sacrament can convincingly carry time into eternity with the authority our souls long for. This is not meant as any kind of substitute for more orthodox ways of celebrating Advent; it simply represents one congregation's attempt to express itself in a way that was personal to itself. If it manages to encourage other groups to experiment in the same way, using their own material to do so, it will have succeeded in its aim.

An Advent Liturgy

I

All:	Hymn ('O come, O come, Emmanuel')
Leader:	You want us to wait for you.
	You, the God of minutes, hours and days.
	We must live in wait for you
	And spend our time together doing it.
Voice 1:	You want us to look out for you.
	You, the God of place and space.
	By looking out for one another
	We must be searching everywhere for you.
Voice 2:	You want us to be loving you
	Across the minutes, hours and days
	So that we may learn to be like you
	In loving one another all our time together.
All:	Yours is the loving, the searching, the waiting.
	Without you we have nothing, are nothing.
	You do it in us because you do it for us.
	We commend this dying year to you.

Everybody remains standing in silence for a few seconds, at the end of which all say the Lord's Prayer.

All:	Hymn ('Be Thou my vision, O Lord of my heart')
Leader:	Now let us bring the past year before God silently in

	prayer, asking the Holy Spirit to guide us and help us remember.
All:	We believe in God almighty, creator of heaven and earth . . .

II

A bell is sounded three times

Dancers portray the ending of the old and beginning of the new. It is a slow dance in which each person is carrying a slender pole. Starting at the circumference of a circle, they move into the centre and out again, miming a battle of staves, as in a traditional Morris dance. Finally, they form into two opposing teams, one of which forces the other into retreat, and then disperse. The movement is stately rather than aggressive, and the music solemn and melodious. The staves are used for pushing, not prodding!

III

The bell sounds twice

Leader:	'It is now the moment for us to wake from sleep,
All:	For salvation is nearer to us now than when we first became believers.'
All:	Hymn ('Morning has broken')
All:	Glory to God in the highest, and peace to his people on earth . . .
All:	Our Father, who art in heaven . . .
Voice 1:	(Mtt. 28: 18-20) "And Jesus came . . . I have commanded you."
Voice 2:	(taking over from Voice 1) "And remember, I am with you always, to the end of the age."
All:	(said antiphonally) For everything there is a season, and a time for every matter under heaven . . . a time for war and a time for peace (Ecc. 3).
Leader:	A time for everything. This time is *ours*. So go forth in peace to love and serve the Lord.
All:	In the name of Christ. Amen.

The bell sounds once

Each of the three examples of ad hoc liturgy-making included in this chapter attempts to deal with a case of unfinished business. None of them claims any authority save that of the genre to which they all belong, that of the liturgical expression of human living and dying, what is now almost universally known as the 'rite of passage'. These three passage rites have been specially chosen for variety of theme so far as subject matter is concerned, but this is not the point at issue here. The death of Simon's father, Sally's bank career, the passing of the old year so that the new one may begin – all are situations which call for some kind of acknowledgement; they are all questions which call for some kind of an answer, matters remaining un-addressed. We search for a sense of balance, of *completeness* in life which is frustrated by experiences like this. Our consciousness of them may decay in time, but there is evidence that their mark on our lives remains and that it interferes at a deep level with our happiness, our satisfaction with life.

The last example is the most significant. The rites of passage which stood out so clearly for Van Gennep provide chapter and verse for a fundamental characteristic of human life which had never before been so clearly recognised by locating it in something which has a more powerful effect on our living and dying than anything else, the passage of time. Come what may, the seasons of the year form a regular pattern, whether or not they are publicly marked in any way. The cycle of liturgical observance refers to a need for staging posts within our experience of time which will represent for us the course of our human experience. For this the passing seasons are a model which we cannot ignore, provided for us by the world in which we "live, move and have our being". More than this, they are a prototype of personal meaning, a pattern of human purpose bestowing a divine symmetry on their earthly life in Christ Jesus.

To summarise what we have discovered about liturgy from our exploration of rites of passage within a Christian framework:

1   The ritual nature of liturgy reveals it as an acted statement about life change which affirms human belief in the possibility of self-transcendence. This is because:

2   ritual carries us back into the world of dramatic representation associated with religious observance from the very

earliest of times – a world still available to us in liturgical form.

3   Working liturgically in the way we have been describing helps us to refresh our awareness of liturgical truth at the dramatic source of liturgy itself, by re-discovering it as a form of action.

Words are used here, certainly, but not in the way that groups of people usually use them – for discussion, for argument, for description, as the subject matter of talks and lecture series. These words are testimony to present experience within the world contained by, created by, the liturgy; they are words used to further the action, language as demonstration. Their purpose is to make a picture of life more life-like than it would be if absolutely nothing at all were said. People speak, and what they say is part of the liturgical action. The way they say it, however, *is* that action, in the workshop as in liturgical action itself: word is gesture and gesture, word.

All this is simply a way of bringing home the essential purpose and significance of what is being said here. Ritual celebration, ritual demonstration, ritual games – all are aspects of ritual used in order to discover the truth of a dramatic situation, inspired by the scenario in which it takes place and to which it contributes, as worshippers try out liturgy for size, relating it to their own knowledge of the story to which it belongs, and to which it lends its own particular weight.

I believe it is essential to experiment in this way in order to transform our current liturgical practice by putting the heart back into our worship at the place where we feel the lack of it most painfully – at the interface between our own personal life situations and our sense of God. Here, on the frontier, is where we most need a living liturgy, one which is rooted in our personal experience of being human by responding in a way which gives shape to our lives, allowing the past to die and be reborn for us.

Writing some years ago I remember saying that

the continuing sense of a dead person's presence is usually explained as a kind of psychological denial, a way in which the self defends itself against a violently traumatic experience. As such it represents a benevolent mitigation of reality, a necessary cushioning of a blow which might otherwise prove totally insupportable. (1988a, p. 26)

When I wrote this I was working full time as a hospital chaplain, and as such coming into frequent contact with other people's bereavement. In those days I was concerned with the state of mind of people who were generally considered to be emotionally wounded. I wrote as a professional, standing apart from the experiences I was describing, in order to gain the necessary objectivity to describe them; and I was at pains to point out that such a reaction "was not a sign of mental breakdown, but a protection against the threat of such a breakdown". People in parishes, whether ordained or lay, may not always see things in such a way or write so dispassionately about them.

The fact remains that, in this case as in so many others, a clinical situation serves to focus a particular state of affairs which exists far beyond the confines of 'scientific medicine'; a state of affairs with which medical or psychiatric ways of understanding are only one way of approaching the business of being human and the extremes of personal experience involved in our painful and precarious journeying through life. Seen from this point of view, rites of passage provide a type of specialised healing, help of the most personal kind. Liturgy, like the process of diagnosis, treatment and aftercare is a way of dealing with a frontier situation – the frontier between life and death. Just as an un-dressed wound or an untreated illness is a piece of human business demanding to be addressed, so is the witness of an unquiet mind, one which is severely troubled by a sense of being burdened with guilt or remorse, or both. In George Herbert's words:

Love bade me welcome: yet my soul drew back
Guiltie of dust and sin . . .

Faith experiences this as more than simply a feeling of unworthiness to live – or die – in God's presence. This is a genuine condition, an intolerable way of being, a question which must be answered; it is an obstacle that has to be removed so the life-passage is restored. Faith, even the strongest, needs not merely assurance, but *reassurance.*

Our liturgies are a means of reassurance. We need more than something we are told, a message transmitted to us. We ourselves must take part in the transmission, and do so in the most whole-hearted way we can. To do this we must know that it is God's purpose for us: we are actively invited to participate within the forgiveness event, and enabled, in Christ, to do so:

> And know you not, says Love, who bore the blame?
>   My deare, then I will serve.
> You must sit down, says Love, and taste my meet.
>   So I did sit and eat.

Herbert is, of course, writing about the Eucharist; but what he says is true of all liturgical action. For Christians – and for other people of faith – the meal is archetypal of our relationship with God who welcomes us into fellowship. In the liturgy of taking, breaking and sharing, the actions which constitute the definitive act of partic-ipation, all our human business is achieved.

This, then, is *the drama of the rite* – the chosen mode of God's revelation, the inclusive–exclusive event: not a message but a happening, a divine play which calls upon a sacred history but is itself a living presence, the scenario of ultimate transformation.

Such is the original from which our passage ceremonies are derived and draw their force. Even when they do not explicitly present the actions of Christ and his disciples, they embody an intention to meet and share – to meet *for* sharing – which is the sign of a spiritual grace because the purpose it represents is sacramental. From this point of view liturgies are eucharists as much as eucharists are liturgies. Participating in Christ is always our purpose. We do it eagerly, not just to give expression to its meaning, but to satisfy our yearning for more than our finitude can bear, an end which is not merely closure but fulfilment of purpose.

It is not only Christians who feel like this, of course. The study of religions throughout the world shows that human beings every-where, and at all periods of history – and pre-history – felt the necessity to express such a longing. The dramatic, or dramatising, impulse to present a picture of how we live and die lies alongside the spiritual need to reach out to what we believe lies beyond. Which came first remains a matter for academic discussion, some of it based in anthropological speculation. For our purposes, questions of chronology or primacy of effect seem comparatively pointless. Liturgies may be seen as theological dramas, or theatre as the arena for travel within the realm of the spirit; the fact remains that throughout the world religious faith finds expression in the enactment of ceremonies whose intention is metaphysical as distinct from instrumental, aiming at celebration rather than manipulation – except of course insofar as the experience of final meaningfulness, an overarching and conclusive significance of human gesture is purposive behaviour . . .

But these expressive ceremonies are always celebrations of something which has happened, rather than techniques used in order to make it happen. They invoke a completeness already experienced, a landscape already travelled. They are repeatable because they are assurances of a consummation previously established, by means of which eternity is present 'within' the signification of home-coming and renewal; what Eliade refers to as the "Myth of the Eternal Return" (1955), which we might also characterise as the mythic embodiment of an unconquered faithfulness, an immediacy of beyond-ness, known in the action of reaching out *and nowhere else*: the significant gesture of transformation.

What, then, is the drama of the rite? It is the spirit in which it is offered, one of responsiveness to the call to move beyond, to journey into beyondness, and the language of imagination in which the journey is to be carried through. It is the drama of departure realised in the spirit of arrival, of an exposition which holds within it the promise of a final denouement as the seed retains the blueprint of the flower – yet never so surely, for this encoding is of faith not sight. As the play carries the pledge of realistic action and truthful experience, so the rite participates in the actuality of its message, its message *as* actuality, experienced in the shape of a repeatable liturgy engrafted through faith within our continuing life together.

VI | Liturgy and Transformation

The aim of liturgy is to glorify God. Its function is to liberate change and then to embrace it. But first it must be encountered, recognised, faced up to. This means allowing it to be itself. Change must be permitted to change . . .

Again, the purpose of liturgy is to release and not to bind. Students of ritual have laid stress on the ability of ceremony and symbolic enactment to tame centrifugal impulses, whether personal or social, by enclosing them or at least the idea of them within the structure of a definite event, something specially put together for purposes of 'containment', a statement or message with a beginning, a middle and an end, in which the middle part is capacious and robust enough to withstand any kind of disorder of thought or feeling assigned to it and simply bring it into agreement with the surrounding sense. Rites of passage have been seen as social mechanisms for the restoration of conformity at times when the forces of nature and/or the human psyche threatened to get out of hand. Certainly they do have this calming effect in the long run, and it is quite usual to see them as safe ways of allowing people to let off steam in the interest of social control. As we have seen, this is to misunderstand the nature of such occasions, which actually change individual experience, and consequently affect human society at a fundamental level, by encouraging changes in the way we think about ourselves and the roles we are prepared to play among our fellow women and men – either by breaking new ground or preserving sources of nourishment threatened by destructive social change. The action of the rite is to invoke a more powerful presence than the dominant social structure. In order to affect it in such a context the presence invoked is experienced as disruptive, threatening the status quo – a chaotic force able to move mountains and to shift the ground on which the city has been constructed.

This is necessary anarchy. Human society must change in order to live. It is, after all, *human* society. Something as basic to individuals as the need for change and development must play its part in their social organisation too. At this level the social-control view of liturgical expression begins to make sense; in order to continue to exist, individuals, families, communities, social systems must overcome their natural resistance to change, and this cannot be encompassed by gentle persuasion. The meaning and significance of ritual abides in the incursive life which it sets out to control and cannot. Certainly it can moderate its impact, but in doing so it actually increases its effectiveness. Human beings are not equipped to deal with that much otherness. We need to be transformed in ways we can cope with; but it is the rite which changes us, not we who make use of it as a way of preserving the *status quo ante.*

Religious ritual cannot really be used to correct social discontinuities or breakdowns in the structure of personal relationships in any way which is directly instrumental. The most it can do is counterbalance social lesions and organisational weaknesses by its specific reference to, and realisation of, a spiritual reality running parallel to – and underlying – the social one. Its relationship with social structure is one of dialogue rather than homology; and the same is true of psychological theory and practice. Social structure articulates societies, and psychological theory formulates ideas about the mental life of individuals. The structural meaning of ritual is intrinsic to itself and has no essential exterior reference either to sociology or psychology.

Ritual is the native tongue of religious awareness. When it speaks, it speaks of itself. It witnesses to its own reality and truthfulness – which is to say that it speaks to us of God, for it is in the rite that we become aware of God as he acts in the world of men and women, God as he is *for us.*

Ritual speaks through its actions, not its words. It is no kind of explanation, but a direct presentation of religious reality. Words cannot help but explain something or other, and the explanation is rarely good enough. As far as the relationship of God and man is concerned, it is never good enough! George Steiner has reminded us of the unreliability of words when it comes to describing the ultimate truth of being: "Words distort; eloquent words distort absolutely." The rite does not depend on words but on the transforming actions of lived life. It is these actions, the human experiences of change and growth, that are recognised and validated by our encounter with God in the Christian sacraments. Their identity as rites of passage renders the sacraments the perfect embodiment of the message implicit in the Gospel narrative, in the nature of the Gospel *as* narrative, a description of the life, death and resurrection of the 'word made flesh'. The gospels describe a God who shared the experiences of a particular generation of men and women, lived in a particular place, at a particular time, was subject to a very specific set of social, political, religious and economic circumstances. At the same time Jesus the man passed through every vitally significant stage which characterises the process of human growth and development. As with every other human being, it was precisely this journeying through life that constituted his essential nature as a person. Without this he could not have been human – for humanness is manifested in time and change, in the dynamic processes of existence. This being so, the ideal theophany for the people of God, the true sacrament of the Body of Christ, can be no other than the establishment and perfecting of men and women as creatures that are continually changing, as they must always be growing and learning. This fact in itself establishes the nature of sacraments as rites of passage in which the time-bound nature of human life is recognised and established in the very process which transforms it. This fundamental message of the sacramental rite of passage needs no words, is implicit in the actual form of the ritual itself. It is the shape of the rite – the shape it *possesses* and that it *allows* – that speaks.

Liturgy is the ally of changes in the way that people and societies come to regard life. Its function is countervailant, and the statement it makes cuts across any other messages we may be receiving in time, making impossible things possible, over-riding the chaos of our communication systems with a message whose simplicity confounds our frantic sense-making. From this point of view liturgical action is not so much a container but an arena; a place of exposure and confrontation, in which all our gestures are taken up in an overarching offering of truth about ourselves – our doubts and uncertainties, our anger and confusion, our faith and our hopelessness. Sure enough its form symbolises the promise of meaning – but a very different meaning from that which constitutes its content. It is the balance between form and content, containment and exposure, which makes it a practical tool for us to use. Do this in remembrance of me. The gift of liturgy makes encounter humanly possible.

The world of the victim of drastic existential change is not only emotionally disrupted it is also cognitively shattered. He or she searches for metaphors to assimilate an experience which cannot be perceived in literal terms as the simple description of events, but requires the language of symbolism in which thought and feeling are united in the effort to be as specific as possible about matters which defy objective analysis. Events in life, stories of things that actually happened or are believed to have happened, become material for symbolic statements around which a subsistent universe of discourse can be organised. Soon after her husband was killed in tragic circumstances, a bereaved woman was lying in the bed they had shared when the ceiling of the room began to fall on her. For months and years afterwards she could only think about what had befallen her in terms of this event. The incident provided her with a way of ordering her awareness of present and future: the ceiling became the foundation of her work of reconstruction. A man who had lost his wife became ill himself each time her dog grew sick. When finally the beloved pet died he broke down completely for a short time, but the dog's death allowed him to think more clearly about his loss (you might say it defined its nature as total), and so contributed to his eventual recovery.

Such stories are very numerous. Bereaved people long for some kind of message from a confused and seamless universe which will allow the processes of conceptual thought – thought which functions through the generation of an endless series of pregnant conclusions – to reassert themselves. The almost universal feelings of guilt which accompany bereavement and which are customarily explained as disguised anger according to the Freudian model, emerge here as the cognitive unease associated with unfinished business of a personal and pressing nature: chances that have been missed, debts left unhonoured, promises broken, vital messages not sent, all occasions of discord which now seem to be established irrevocably. In this situation "things done cannot be undone"; and if there was no bitterness but only acceptance and love, then there could never be *enough* love shown to the beloved in the time allowed, and the bereaved person is left tormented by the thought of 'if only'" 'if only I had said this, if only I had done that', perpetually searching for the answer to a problem which eludes and torments. We seek out the dead in order to have the blessed relief of talking to them again, so that they may really know what we thought and felt about them. From this point of view, funeral services are ways in which we hand our message on to God so that he may 'put the dead person in the picture' and ease our own cognitive frustration. The funeral embodies a conscious intention on our own part to proclaim a straightforward message about the dead, and its function is to promote an even greater consciousness. The way in which we express our thoughts and feelings about the dead in funeral liturgies tells us a great deal about the nature of ritual itself.

Liturgy then is a gift which allows us to move onwards through life. This is what we say, and we are used to saying it. From the Apostolic age it has been part of the staple diet of Christians that the sacraments are food for our journey through life. Spiritually speaking, this is the nourishment which we expect and over the centuries have depended on for the continuance of our journey, so that, at a basic level of our corporate awareness we tend to see it as a bland, familiar diet. This is to underestimate both God and his chosen way of addressing us. We are not just fed by liturgy; we are weaned by it. In it we are brought face to face with the fact that there are various kinds of food for this journey, and that some of it is much less digestible than we would like it to be. The function of ritual initiation is to enable us to benefit from the kind of sustenance which we naturally find hard to swallow because it is not what we would have chosen for ourselves.

If we wish to move forwards as individuals in community into a deeper and fuller inheritance of our redeemed being as the people of God, the greatest obstacle in our path is the fact of human conflict. I say that this is the worst difficulty facing us because it gets in the way of the most precious ability human beings possess – the ability to *share* the problems, difficulties, barriers to communication, defeats and opposing triumphs, where the symbolic reality we proclaim in liturgy are worked though in the experience of sharing. In the rite, this is how these things come to be tackled – not by ignoring them (or as we would prefer it, finding a way in which they can be shelved out of sight in some convenient storehouse of the human spirit) but by living through a shared experience of human limitations and divine deliverance.

If liturgy's task is to express the victory of love in and through conflict, then surely it must be allowed to take the reality of inter-personal conflict into its orbit and be allowed to find its own way of dealing with it. What it certainly should not be used for is avoidance of conflict. At the level of individual problems and difficulties this principle has not always been accepted. Christians confess their sins – to one another or to a representative of the Church – and then proceed to bring their wounds to God for healing in the action of Holy Communion. In a very real sense, however, this is a way of avoiding the issue; not for the person themselves, but for the congregation as a whole (and consequently for him or her as members of the congregation). Liturgy is basically about our participation in one another. Wounds which constitute what Lionel Thornton called "the common life in the Body of Christ" (1963).

This is not the way we often use it, however. In all the major disputes within the Church liturgy is employed to boost one or other side of the argument in order to reinforce the spiritual – and hence moral – superiority of a particular position. If liturgy is 'used' like this it will always weigh the scales in favour of orthodoxy against any kind of innovative position, so that change within the life of the Church as a whole, or of any particular congregation, will be slowed down rather than encouraged. Somehow or other we have to find ways of letting liturgy speak on behalf of the miraculous transfor-mation it represents, so that those involved are reminded of the abiding need for change to be lived as part of the human condition – constitutive of being human rather than an unfortunate reminder of the limitations attached to life in the present. It is *because* we have arrived that we have the courage to move forward.

In this way, liturgy is intrinsic to the process of living our beliefs about the nature of the Church, as eternal and temporal, human and divine, flesh and Word. Our liturgies enflesh our understanding of truth by presenting it to us as dialectical, the outcome of a struggle for change, a wind that blows through the structures of churches – *blows where it wills*. Liturgy enacts the struggle rather than the solution; or rather it reveals the struggle in terms of the solution, embodying Spirit-on-the-move. Elaine Graham has drawn attention to the role of liturgy in expressing aspects of Christian understanding which are neglected or were suppressed as theologically irrelevant:

> Truly liberative liturgy will not be exclusive; [it will seek] to encompass all human experience and community life as worthy and redemptive. Christian worship at its most individual and honest, is thus one of the practical embodiments in word and deed, of the primary values and truth claims of the Christian faith. (in Williams and Swindon, 2000: 100)

Its value, however, depends on its honesty in living up to its own nature as proclaimer of the truth about individuals and societies, revealing their limitations and needs, sharing the facts about their problems, including their interpersonal disagreements and the impassioned disputes arising out of them. It is not possible for liturgy to be honest about the states of affairs it describes without first being honest about itself, its own nature as the symbolism of a clash of forces out of which a new kind of truth emerges. In order to do this it must be willing to proclaim itself as problem, not merely solution. This means that in the confrontation which lies at its heart, both sides should be fairly represented.

Graham cites the facts about human sexuality as examples of areas in life which the Church refuses to treat as problematic, having decided beforehand what the answer will be, and sticking to this even though it does not really do justice to the situation with regard to actual human experience. As Stuart points out, "For the liturgy to be effective it needs to articulate and speak to the experience of those who take part in it, in word and symbol" (1992, p. 11). He is writing as editor of *A Gay and Lesbian Prayer Book*, and issues of human sexuality do certainly account for a considerable proportion of the disputed territory within contemporary Christianity. There are other things about which Christians disagree, however, one of them being the metaphorical nature of Christian texts – how far are they be to taken literally and to what extent are they open to interpretation? All such disagreements represent a falling away from the truth of Christians belonging only to the extent that they represent questions which may not be asked and answers which have already been finally given in ways which cannot permit any kind of argument, particularly those drawing attention to changed situations and circumstances; answers which deny the existence of any kind of problem at all. If our liturgies are to be the embodiment of our awareness of God, they must take particular care in showing us as we are, not as we would like to be, free from our doubts and fears, and the resentful anger we sometimes feel if we fail to convince others that our own position is the right one, the only genuine Christian one.

In practical terms this means working liturgically to express our disunities, because this is what liturgy is *for*; if what we are looking for is a way of proclaiming a built-in consensus we should avoid this dialectical way of expressing ourselves. As Graham asserts, rites are ways of expressing theologically suppressed aspects of human need, experiences which resist rationalisation into one or another kind of formula. The dramatic, confrontational, nature of liturgy allows both sides of a conflict situation to be presented without argument as an image of a problem faced and worked through, in which apparently intractable oppositions are lived out in the name of a truth which is precisely the opposite of the conclusions we are accustomed to draw from the situations we find ourselves in. The biblical text for such a liturgy would be the beatitudes, and its central image the resurrection of the dead in Jesus Christ.

Deprived of its dramatic armature, its language of logical self-contradiction, liturgy ceases to have any value as a unique way of saying things which cannot otherwise be said; things about Spirit which every kind of literal description reduces to a lifeless imitation, the denial of the truth it is trying to establish, the living transforming truth which is so much more than winning an argument. If we live the liturgy, by the time we have lived it through we shall discover that we have moved away from confrontation into something much more like acceptance – the acceptance of differences in which relationship subsists. In liturgy the imagery of love creates love; congregations are to be encouraged to share their differences regarding the Church using the language provided by the Church to do so.

It is not hard to see how important this is at a time when acted worship – liturgy – is almost universally regarded as only acceptable in contexts of agreement, because of the danger that it may so easily become a way of disguising the truth instead of revealing and celebrating its fullness.

Offering up the Struggle

If we wanted to construct such a liturgy, how would we set about it? Here is an example of how one congregation did it.

A. Stage One

In this stage were readings, music, movement, all setting forth the reality which confronted us, the situation as we saw it – *i.e.* the terms of the disagreement – in as authoritative a way as possible. For our congregation this meant choosing two texts, one from the bible (Jesus' beatitudes), the other a prayer for peace ('Lord make us instruments of thy peace . . . '), plus a short address in dialogue form focusing their specific relevance to the conflict envisaged in the action of the rite.

B. Stage Two

At the centre, in the liturgy's second phase, no words were spoken. This part consisted of the iconography in acted form of the struggle itself – waves beating at the cliff's foot, a mountain torrent expending its force against the roots of a solitary tree, actions in which one half of the congregation pitted its strength against the other to no apparent avail. From time to time the centre of the action shifted as new versions of the theme of struggle and resistance emerged, dividing up the participants in a variety of new ways. Out of this chaos, at the climax, the leader called everyone together into a wide circle where they stood facing one another. Now hold hands, she said . . .

C. Stage Three

Still holding hands, people sang together some of the songs they loved singing. Quietly they invoked Christ's presence, 'the peace which passeth all understanding'. People spoke and prayed aloud, others stood in silence celebrating a love which conquers every attempt we make to stand in its way. At length, when everyone fell silent, we simply shared the silence together as the pledge of the desire for reconciliation as a victory gained by both sides – "the glorious liberty of the children of God".

This liturgy-drama had a lasting effect on the people taking part in it, who sometimes refer to it as a turning point in the life of the congregation. All in all we got a lot out of it. We certainly put a lot in; this stands out clearly in the bald description given above. Certainly the dramatic language was familiar to a lot of us, having been involved in the creation of experimental liturgies over a number of years. If people are not used to this kind of approach the dramatic nature of what takes place needs to be adapted so that they do not feel over-stretched by doing (and saying) things they can't remember having been involved in before – not in church, at any rate! Often this is a matter of personal involvement at what at first seems to be an unacceptable level for public worship. People who say this, or something like it, should be treated with great respect. The drama implicit in Christian liturgy is always capable of having an effect on people's emotions, and some people find this very embarrassing. This can happen in the most restrained services, where a discreet tear can be swiftly wiped away when nobody else is looking. In services like this, discretion has to work harder and it may well prove a losing battle. It is therefore doubly important that those invited to take part are given the option of refusing to do so; or choosing which parts they want to opt out of, or simply sitting back and watching. After all, that is what you do when you go to see a play; and your best efforts to remain aloof tend not to be as successful as you may at first have intended they should be. Drama has always been a good way of stirring things up!

Because of the role which it, the liturgical genre itself, plays in the way human beings express and communicate their most important, most characteristic, experiences, a liturgy cannot avoid being dramatic. To isolate a meaning in this way, so that it is recognised as itself rather than simply part of some other argument; to draw attention to the unique identity of an event so that its significance may be preserved as a point well made, a conclusion properly reached, opening the way to new conclusions as yet unreached – this is bound to be a dramatic gesture, whether it be carried out by an individual or a group of people. The shape of liturgy allows it to speak by itself as itself, as rites of passage stand head and shoulder out of the normal course of events as positions established, points well made, allowing us to move on with the business of living. The shape itself expresses the possibility of such meanings, and as such they are a type of real human action – action to express the importance of being human, a paradigm of things which must be recognised because they contribute to the process of making sense of our lives. Liturgy is a statement about being human, given all the weight and definition available to us. *Here we are*, it says. *This is what we mean.* To a very great extent, the rite itself manages to say this for us, and to do so however we ourselves may be thinking or feeling at the time. Liturgies where drama has been intensified by our effects to simplify its action and reveal its power to change our world are, as we have seen, able to work in a paradoxical way by involving us through our emotions in the way that drama does; and this drama is capable of speaking on our behalf to embody our profoundest longings – bringing them home to us not simply as ideas but as presences, events in which we are personally involved. In a world which is exhausted by too many words, in one way or another liturgy demands our attention.

Conclusion

For Christians liturgical expresses the reality at the heart of their shared identity. A body which "contemplates the being of God and the being of the Church with the eye of worship" (Zizioulas 1985:19) speaks the language of God revealed to men and women as Father, Son and Holy Spirit, because for Christians to worship "in the name of God" is not merely to give intellectual assent to this logical proposition about Him but to lay hold upon their baptismal identity as the redeemed daughters and sons of God and sisters and brothers of Christ. Christian liturgy is always far more than a theoretical statement about God, our Personhood and the way in which this is hypostasised: it is a living out of the truth by the persons involved in the way that this truth is itself lived out. Certainly it can be done half-heartedly, in ignorance of its reality, but if it is done by baptised Christians it is always the image of the communion between Father Son and Holy Spirit. Just as God is Love, and love must be personal, or the word should not be used at all, so the embodiment of redeemed human-ness in worshipful action is the most personal way of interacting – of *being ourselves in one another* – that we have as human beings; personal enough to be offered to God on behalf of men and women who have either not yet heard the message or not been able to give it their intellectual assent.

From the point of view of human psychology, liturgy is by far the most personal theological experience because it involves sharing with other people. It is not just about sharing, it is in itself a sharing. It does not seek to make itself acceptable on grounds of logical – or theological – analysis of the elements comprising it; it does not stand back from itself at all, because it is involved in reaching out to the other in the power of the Other working in it and manifesting itself through it. Its theology is not one of 'nature' or 'substance' but personal existence – God's as well as the other persons involved.

"Salvation", says Zizioulas, "is identified with the realization of personhood in man" (1985, p. 50). In liturgy personhood expresses itself in acknowledging the source of its own being within the Relationship of Persons which is the Being of God.

This is the purpose and identity of Christian worship, to be relationship offered in celebration of Relationship. Consequently all acts of worship carried out in a spirit of love given and received – a spirit of *interchange* – assume the identity of liturgy itself. The workshops described here all require some development in order to be used liturgically; this is obvious enough. All the same, because they are about the personal action of sharing they lend themselves to being shaped into a more ceremonial, consciously liturgical form, so that the spirit they embody may be focused upon the call to worship and the shared life they present recognise itself as the self-giving of God the Father. As we have seen, the identity of ritual as drama stands out most clearly in rites of passage; but all incorporate ceremonials are in fact scenarios of personal relationship, whether the *dramatis personæ* are human or divine, or, in most cases, both. Christian liturgy goes further and deeper however, for here the drama is not simply presented but *realized*, for those involved are not *personæ* but actual persons, sharers in the creative and sustaining free personhood of God.

The Eucharist was regarded by Christians during the first centuries as a drama whose scenario was realized by Holy Spirit, the action of communion affirming those taking part as members of the Body of Christ. In the light of this Eucharistic sharing, liturgies are icons of the Church's presence in the world. This is to use 'icon' in its true sense as a portrayal of a reality which enshrines its own presence – a medium signifying immediately, which is the way in which the Greek Fathers used it. What is seen, heard and felt here is a liturgical action, just as whatever happens in theatre is indisputably a play. The portrayal of Christian belonging receives its authenticity because those taking part are Christians – men women and children who participate in the Personhood of Father, Son and Holy Spirit. Just as a play is authentically a play because the actors and their audiences are human beings involved in showing forth the terms of their own human belonging, their participation in human-ness. It is what is being shared here which distinguishes liturgy from theatre, the quality of the belonging rather than the action of sharing. Liturgy transcends drama but does not ever deny its importance as the language human beings use to embody their relatedness. If liturgy proclaims a new belonging drama demonstrates exactly what it is that has been transformed.

The best example of all is of course the Eucharist itself, the proto-typical Christian liturgy, embodying as it does Christ's command to "do this is remembrance of me". The action of the Eucharist speaks of Christ's presence as an act of worship is transformed by identification with actions transforming reality itself – the death, Resurrection and Ascension of Christ – so that, in the event, memory becomes presence, becomes immediacy, and the world continues to be transformed. There is no distance in this remembering, for those who take it to heart. This is not simply a matter of our accepting theological instruction – we need to know, not only that these things are, but also that they are *for us*. Eucharistic liturgy brings home realities which no text book can teach. In this case the liturgical action bears the seal of Christ himself; the actual 'shape of the rite', however reveals 'the Church's awareness of the significance of liturgy as the most powerful way of articulating truth which is timeless.

"Festivals take place in Eternity". This was the French Sociologist Marcel Mauss's way of explaining the action of religious rituals in renewing human existence by passing through states of shared experience in which the power of time to control human affairs is temporarily suspended – to be, in fact, rites of passage (1909: 190). For Christians this has a very specific reference indeed. John Zizioulas, for example, drawing on the writings of the Greek Fathers, regards Eucharist as the central experience of Christian life, the theological rock upon which the Church itself is founded. "The Church", he tells us, "has bound every one of her acts to the Eucharist," for it is here that we are alive in a unique way, one which "transcends every exclusiveness of a biological or social kind. In the action of the Eucharist we are no longer circumscribed by our own individuality, and yet our existence as people is established; we are uniquely in communion", delivered to one another and ourselves in a relationship of "free and universal love" (1985: 60). This is a very ancient and well established understanding of the Eucharist as

Patristic theology: "the historical realization of the philosophical principle which governs the concept of the person, the principle that the hypostasis expresses the whole of its nature and not just a past" (1985, p. 60). Here in the Eucharist we are present as body, self and other, future and past, because we are present with Christ.

Here then is the underlying message of this book concerning the importance to the Church of its own liturgies. Wherever the name and presence of Holy Spirit is invoked, even when the liturgical action itself is spontaneous, or even crude in its expression, there is Eucharist. Liturgies open a new world to us; they are future orientated. This is because Christ is here with us in the Eucharistic identity of the liturgical action, its nature as communion, whatever may be its particular ecclesiastical 'credentials'. It is the action of passing through Christ's eternal presence which makes it so, and doing it in person as members of his Mystical Body. The Greek Fathers of the Church identified the life of Christians with the communion which exists between them to the point of seeing God himself as the sharing of Persons, so that "life is imparted and actualised only in an event of communion", for "it is only in relationship that identity appears as having an ontological significance" (Zizioulas 1985: 82, 88). The precedence of worship over doctrine is historical, in the sense that central doctrines concerning the nature of church and sacrament are rooted in the action and experience of Holy Communion itself (Cullman, 1953). Such, for Christians, is the importance of liturgy.

In themselves, then, liturgies are able to reflect the Kingdom, as Christians in communion with One-Who-Is-Communion, work dialectically 'between the already and the not yet,' palpably in the world yet essentially *beyond* it, able through the force of Holy Spirit to carry the world *with* it. In the experience of Christians, liturgies are always sacramental occasions when Christ's presence is acknowledged, either explicitly in word and sign, or implicitly because of what it feels like when he is with us, an experience of being at once held and set in motion, comforted and inspired, accepted and challenged, which we recognise for what it is without question or the possibility of argument, a wonder made all the more amazing by the ordinariness of its surroundings.

The purpose of liturgy is most clearly revealed when its nature is a place of personal sharing, and the journey jointly undertaken is allowed to determine the form it takes. These things have a value for human beings which can hardly be exaggerated. Together they represent the deepest yearnings of the human heart, and in themselves they call out for the kind of answers which argument alone cannot supply us with. From this point of view liturgy is an act of faith, a gesture asserting the presence of the peace "which passes understanding"; but it is also the strongest evidence as to the ultimate triumph of that peace dwelling among us as Word made flesh.

Peace and acceptance. The reason for concentrating on worship as drama is in fact reconciliation. In theatre, which is the embodiment of drama, we are drawn to the other across the distance separating our world from that of the play. In liturgy this separation functions in the distance between ourselves and God, in what Martin Buber calls "the stern over-againstness of I and Thou" (1957, p. 66). Both liturgy and theatre work dialectically in order to express and promote a relationship of difference. Theatre is a paradigm of ritual, a coming together of realities which are normally both experienced and understood as being opposites – what Jung refers to as a *coincidentia oppositorum* (in McGuire and Hull 1978, p. 328). It is in this coming together of separateness that relationship itself consists; it is an encounter, not a fusion, because the new relational reality preserves and ratifies and establishes identity.

In religious rituals we have a sense of meeting God. In the case of rites of passage and initiations, this is a genuine human experience affecting our lives as human beings; indeed it is the most important thing about our lives. Ritual 'seen from the inside' has a particular effect on us, as all passionate encounters do. As the anthropologist Van der Leeuw pointed out, "the virtue of a religion is not in its texts but its effects" (1938). Ritual takes our minds off who we are: we lose our self-consciousness and throw ourselves into the arms of the Beloved. While this is going on we forget about differences, even ultimately significant ones, and enjoy what we experience as a timeless moment of union.

Finally, there are two main reasons for valuing the drama of worship. First, it allows the ritual symbol to retain its metaphorical force and point beyond itself to what is, literally speaking, unattainable. In this way it allows us to enter into relation with a reality which is perceptually outside our range and cannot be known by mere description, or even illustration. Indeed, the more expressive it is, the more it encourages us to confuse symbolism with the straightforward transfer of identity. However we approach liturgy, it surely must never be as a process in which people are brought psychologically into a frame of mind in which they are able to accept the truth of their union with Christ without surprise, without a sense of the impossibility of that which has taken place by faith.

Second, it brings home the experience of forgiveness and acceptance as something which takes place in the encounter *between* persons. The gospel message about reconciliation with God is expressed in terms of forgiveness, as something to be passed on, spiritually present in every personal encounter, embodying the essence of personhood itself. To be in relation with someone else is implicitly to accept them and to be accepted by them. Even when forgiveness is not explicitly called for, such acceptance carries a relational requirement. In rite, as in theatre, the fundamental gesture is one of exchange, a reaching out toward the Other in an exchange of awareness. For human beings, this involves not fusion but sharing, the interchange of love. In Holy Communion, Christ establishes God's acceptance by sharing himself with sinners so that they too may share themselves. Both being accepted by the other, and the acceptance of the other, are of God.

Appendix 1:
Kris's Service

Kris was a cat from the west coast of Ireland – Achill Island in Co. Mayo. We brought him back to England when he was still very small, as a way of rescuing him from the Bank Holiday motorbikes which were rushing at idiotic speeds through Keel village. The house where he was born was an old coastguard station overlooking Keel Strand – almost on the strand, as a matter of fact; from the windows you can look down four miles of curving beach to the Minaun Cliffs – indescribable, so I won't try.

We smuggled Kris out of Ireland in a shoe box because we didn't know what the Irish Ferries people would say about carrying cats out of Ireland. We reserved a cabin for him, something we don't bother doing for ourselves, and he spent the entire crossing trying to destroy the mattress on the bunk, but since he was only about eight inches long, I don't think he did any permanent damage. He lived happily in England for the usual span of years permitted to cats (without being run over) and grew into an exceedingly handsome and noble animal. It seems to us that he died before his time.

When he died we buried him with the other cats we'd known and loved, in the garden. But as soon as we could manage it, we went back to where he was born – where he *should* have lived his life (and would have done if it hadn't been for those motorbikes) and set up a simple memorial using a large shiny stone from the beach. It is still there; every year when we go back to Keel Strand we make sure of this, although sometimes we have to rescue it from where it has been moved by the receding tide. This is the memorial service we said for Kris on the beach at Achill Island.

Liturgy for a Beloved Animal

I

All: King of Glory, King of Peace.

Minister: Trust me: there are many dwelling places in my Father's house.

The Lord be with you.

All: And also with you.

Minister: You create wonders, Father, and share them with us. For you, creating and sharing are the same thing. You are Love, and love is what you make; you give us love for the loving, and we love what you have made. Most of all, we love the living things you make. People and animals – animals who are like people to us – we share among us the love which never ends. Amen.

Poems by D. H. Lawrence ("All that matters is to be at one with the Living God"), Robin Skelton and Christopher Smart are read.

Minister: We have come here to give thanks for one of our family, Kris the cat. Kris was born here, near this beach. We remember what he looked like – lithe and awkward, wild and gentle, the spirit of Achill Island making itself gentle out of love for us. We remember how he was towards us and give thanks to God for the 17 years he spent with us. As much as a cat can (and who knows how much that is?) Kris knew how much we loved him, and he opened his heart to us in return. Now he climbs higher trees in another place, for being at rest doesn't mean just doing nothing at all: it means being yourself as you really are, as God created you to be, free from the limitations of life here. At the same time he is still here with us. His presence, not merely a memory, lives here. It is part of what will always be between us.

All: 'All creatures of our God and King'

II

Kris's picture is passed round the congregation and everybody recalls incidents in his life or says something that they remember about him. When this has finished, the pictures and any other mementoes are taken and laid on the table. After a pause the Lord's Prayer is said.

All: Our Father . . .

III

All: Hymn ('Be Thou my vision')

Minister: That is what he was like. Now we have said goodbye to him in the place that gave him birth. It was a privilege to have him with us.

All: Benedicite ('O earth bless the Lord: you cattle and wild beasts, sing his praises, exalt him for ever')

Minister: Lord of all, we remember Kris in your presence. We commend him in all his ways to you. We part in love as we lived together in love. Help us to keep his memory fresh in our hearts and to show our love for him in the way we regard all those creatures with whom we share your world. Through Jesus Christ, our Lord.

All: Amen.

All: Hymn ('Morning has broken')

Minister: Grant, O Father, that we may be reunited in the full knowledge of your love and the unclouded vision of your glory.

All: The grace of our Lord Jesus Christ . . .

Appendix 2:
Some Rite of Passage Outlines

1. The Birth of a Child
A

- Psalm 100
- Introduce the Liturgical theme:
  - a dramatic, pictorial or choreographed presentation of how thing stand at present and the direction you want to go in for the future.
  - a short spoken commentary on the change involved.
- Sing a hymn/song, asking for guidance from God and help carrying through important life changes.

B

- Make contact with somebody sitting or standing near you. What do you find most encouraging about life? What do you find most frightening? Find someone near you to talk to about this.
- Listen quietly as someone reads 'The Annunciation Story' (Luke 1:26–38). This story may be acted out in mime.
- Reflect on the experience of carrying a new life within yourself. Mime passing a 'handful' of water around the congregation. Pray, silently or aloud.
- The child's parents move down to the front, carrying the child. When they arrive there, they turn and face the people, and the mother holds her child out to them. Immediately the Magnificat is said, sung or danced.

C

- After a few moments of quietness, join in singing a hymn of thanksgiving.
- Find some way of expressing how you personally feel about

this new life and the joy it has brought with it. Can you find something to symbolise this?

- Go and congratulate the parents and greet the baby.
- Sing a hymn, psalm or song.
- Hold hands and say goodbye.

The theme here is welcome, acceptance, arrival, the reception of a new human being by the rest of the human race. It is an initiation into the condition of being alive, a human being amongst other human beings. It is a liturgy of bonding, the Church's offering to parents as a gift in celebration of a joyous occasion.

2. A Son's or Daughter's Leaving Home
A

- Psalm 148
- Introduce the Liturgical theme
  (*As Workshop I*).
- Sing a hymn/song.

B

- Find a partner, someone you can talk to about how you felt when you left home for the first time. Join up with another couple and take it in turns to tell them what your partner has told you. (You will need to ask your partner's permission first.)
- As a group of four people, decide what gift you would like to give the person leaving home. How will you symbolise this? Choose someone to represent your group.
- Move into a circle and ask the person leaving home to stand or sit in the middle. Dispatch your group leader to make a solemn presentation of your gift to them.
- Read Matthew 4:1-11.
- The person leaving home receives your symbolic gifts, and responds in any way she/he feels able to. (If they are skilled in any kind of presentation you can encourage them to express themselves in that particular way.)

C

- Sing a hymn or song of farewell.
- Pray together, silently or aloud, for families, nations and the whole world.
- Stand in a circle. Holding hands, say goodbye to the one leaving home. Do this in unison.
- Say goodbye and bless one another.

This workshop resembles the previous one in that its theme is that of setting out into the adult world. It could be used when somebody is setting out for university or embarking on vocational training of some kind; it could be relevant for setting out on a journey towards the achievement of a personal goal. The idea of 'finding one's own way' emerges here, with the confusion which precedes commitment to a particular view of oneself and one's world.

3. Becoming Engaged
A

- Psalm 19.
- Introduce the Liturgical theme:
  (*As Workshop* 1).
- Sing a hymn/song.

B

- Shake hands with people round you, offering them a blessing in any way you and they find comfortable.
- Find some space in which you can sit quietly for a few minutes. Remember a time in your life when you were really happy and life was particularly exciting for you.
- Form a group with people you know, and share your memories with them.
- Invite one of the two engaged people into your group, so that you can ask them how and where they met their partner-to-be, and where and how they decided to get married.
- In a circle, imagine what particular gift you would like to give to the engaged couple. Now ask them to stand together in the centre of the circle so that you take your gift to them

- Read John 2.

C

- Sing a hymn or song of thanksgiving and celebration.
- Create a group prayer, in which each person in the circle adds on their own (short) prayer to the one offered up by the person standing or sitting next to them.
- Spend a few minutes dancing together. Try to find a dance everyone knows.
- After saying goodbye and exchanging blessings, form a crocodile behind the couple and dance out of the doorway.

This workshop corresponds to the pre-liminal role of the extended rite of passage for a marriage. In Catholic and Protestant practices the three stages are telescoped into a single wedding service, but it is doubtful if this is really an improvement; of all the undertakings we make in life, getting married is certainly one of the most considerable ones, involving far-reaching changes in the way we look at ourselves and the world looks at us. Even when we have decided to embark on this journey, we need time to work through the experience of making such a decision.

4. Welcoming a Family into the Congregation
A

- Psalm 100.
- Introduce the Liturgical theme:
  (*See Workshop* 1).
- Sing a hymn/song.

B

- Say hello to people, making sure to greet anybody new to the gathering (particularly the new family).
- Find a space and a piece of paper, and write down as many words as you can think of connected with families and belonging together.
- Join up with other people and compare notes. Which words has everybody got in their list? What ones are unique to you?

- Spread a large piece of paper out on the floor and make a comprehensive list of words, everybody joining in to write, draw or paint on the paper.
- Ask somebody from the new family to read Luke 10:25-37 (The Parable of the Good Samaritan).
- Form a circle in the centre of the space and join hands. Now open the circle up to let the new family join it.

C

- Sing a hymn or song of belonging together.
- In a circle, pray together for families and for those who feel alone in the world.
- Take it in turns to cross the circle and greet the new family.
- Roll the paper up and present it to the newcomers.
- Say goodbye to one another, exchanging blessings for a shared life together.

Some people, when they join a new congregation, prefer to creep in unannounced. However, there comes a time when even these want to feel that they really belong by standing up and being recognised. The workshop is flexible, and intended to be useful for a range of situations like this. For example, it can be adapted to apply to individuals, couples and families at whatever stage of church membership – anybody past the stage of 'sneaking in at the back'.

5. Emigrating
A

- Psalm 23.
- Introduce the Liturgical theme:
  (*See Workshop* 1).
- Sing a hymn/song.

B

- Say hello to as many people as you can, as warmly and personally as possible.
- Paint or draw an image of (or write a short poem about) the place you love best.

- Explore with a partner how it feels to leave home.
- With two other couples, compose a letter (or a song) for the person or people emigrating.
- Read Ruth 1:1-22 (Ruth and Naomi).
- Group by group, hand your letters/poems to the people to whom they are addressed.

C

- In a circle, sing hymns or songs you associate with them, or ones they especially like.
- Still in the circle, invite them to read out any letters or poems they would like to share.
- What memories are they taking away with them? Pause for a moment, then turn outwards, giving those emigrating time to reflect. Encourage them to say anything they feel able to say.
- Join hands and sing a farewell song.
- Say goodbye to everybody – particularly the people or people emigrating.

This is a passage rite in a literal sense, in which ideas of movement and progression correspond to the prospect of a real departure, journey and arrival. Such undertakings deserve to be properly celebrated because of the courage and determination called for from the people involved. The workshop aims to give shape to thoughts and feelings which are still partly unassimilated – whose urgency and shapelessness inhibit us from getting to grips with them. The idea of travelling 'overseas' suggests existential change, because of the metaphor of water as a natural symbol of life emerging from chaos.

6. Saying Goodbye to a Minister
A

- Psalm 114.
- Introduce the Liturgical theme:
  (*See Workshop* 1).
- Sing a hymn/song.

B

- Congregate at one end of the workshop space. Your objective is to make your way across to the other side as if you were moving in darkness and there are obstacles in the way. If you like, you may try to guide someone else but remember that neither of you is supposed to be able to see.
- When you have all reached the other side, congratulate one another with hugs or handshakes. (Sing something if you all feel like it!)
- Gather into groups and find somewhere to sit down together. Will you personally miss the minister? Say in what ways she or he has helped you during their time in office. Pray for him or her.
- In your groups, think of a way in which you express how you feel. Could you act, dance or mime something? Draw or model something? Write a group letter?
- Now ask the minister to sit down somewhere you can all offer your work to her/him.
- Read Matthew 10:5–16 ("As you go, preach this message . . . ").

C

- In a circle, sing one (or more) of the minister's favourite hymns.
- Pray together for the minister (and his/her family) and their ministry in the future.
- Form up into a ceremonial group and lead the minister round the room into the central space. Say goodbye to him/her formally, wishing her/him Godspeed.
- Sing a hymn/song of farewell.

Christian denominations tend to have services for welcoming new ministers, but rarely have any liturgical form of farewell, although individual congregations may arrange something of a formal nature. This workshop concentrates upon the action of saying goodbye as part of a process of meaningful change involving both minister and congregation. It can be adapted in order to include greater awareness of the role of the minister's family in the life of the congregation.

7. Thanksgiving for Recovery from Illness

A

- Psalm 30
- Introduce the Liturgical theme:
  (*See Workshop* 1).
- Sing a hymn/song.

B

- Stand in a circle. Say hello to the people facing you and on each side of you.
- Take it in turns to describe something that has recently happened to you which you would like to share with the group.
- Now turn outwards and take a step forward. Close your eyes and listen hard. Can you hear your heart beating?
- Eyes still closed, explore the space around you until you make contact with someone else. Now reach out and touch their face. Do not speak at all.
- Now open your eyes and move away. Find a piece of paper and somewhere to sit down. What words come into your mind when you think about loving and being loved? If you made an image of caring what would it be like, roughly speaking?
- Leave your paper in the centre of the room. Now form a circle round the papers.
- Read Luke 8:41-56 (Jairus's daughter).

C

- Sing a hymn/song of thanksgiving for healing.
- Pray silently or aloud for all who are sick, or whose lives are in danger. Pray for healers, scientific, spiritual or both, and for carers.
- Take turns to tell or show the one who has recovered how glad you are to see their health restored.
- Give him/her an opportunity to respond in any way they would like to do. Perhaps they, too, would like to contribute to the pile of papers, which can now be offered up to God on behalf of everyone present.

- Say goodbye to everyone, beginning with the person who has recovered.

This is obviously a post-liminal rite (*i.e.* following a hypothetical pre-liminal liturgy of entrance and a liminal period of hospitalisation in between). In this workshop the idea of restoration to personal health is incorporated with that of return to society. This does not necessarily mean that the sick person has been officially segregated from the company of those deemed to be well, although if they have spent time in hospital this may be true; but it does take account of strong feelings on the part of ex-patients of having been somewhat shut away from life. This workshop provides an opportunity to help things back to normal.

8. Asylum and Refuge
A

- Psalm 46
- Introduce the Liturgical theme:
  (*See Workshop* 1).
- Sing a hymn/song.

B

- Wander round the space in silence, until Leader calls a halt.
- Stand or sit where you are
- Leader begins to hum a few bars of an old song. Perhaps someone joins in, or continues the rest of the tune. Leader encourages people to hum old familiar tunes, in their own time, when they come into their minds.
- Take a piece of paper and a pencil, pen or crayon. Write, draw or symbolize a precious person, place or thing from the place you have left behind. If you would like to, show what you have written or drawn to somebody in the group welcoming you. If you want, you can tell them about it.
- Place your paper in the middle of the room.
- Standing in a circle, read Psalm 137, vv. 1–6.

C

- Take one another's hands; following the Leader dance first round the circle, then in a line round the whole space.

- Stopping, turn to face the person next to you and say 'You are welcome'. This is done round the whole circle, as the newcomers welcome their hosts as they too are welcomed. (You may of course exchange hugs, if you aren't too shy or too vulnerable!)
- Sing a hymn or a song which people know, or can easily be taught. Although this can begin in a tentative and informal way, as you sing the version *you* know, and others do the same, it develops more seriously and language differences stop being important.
- In the circle, hold hands and pray, silently or aloud, for those seeking safety and protection in a strange land.
- Before you go, find someone to talk more personally to – perhaps the person who showed you their paper. Say goodbye to each other.

This workshop aims to explore themes which are at the heart of liturgy itself – in other words, human life in an environment perceived as spiritually alien and sometimes actually hostile. It has considerable contemporary relevance – but then it always did have. It can be used when there are no political refugees or asylum seekers within the congregation, but obviously it will have greater impact if some are actually present. However, if this is not possible, the workshop is a powerful reminder of what we share with them and the love we owe them . . .

9. Overcoming Barriers
A

- Psalm 122.
- Introduce a Liturgical Theme:
  (*See Workshop I*).
- Sing a Hymn/Song.

B

- Set yourself an imaginary destination on the opposite side of the room (an architectural feature, a picture, or simply a point in mid-air) and walk determinedly towards it, undeterred by obstacles, human or otherwise. Having arrived, turn round, choose something on the opposite side of the room and do the same again. Continue to do this until Leader calls a halt.

- Find three (or four) other people; decide on a space on the other side of the room which you intend to settle on. Don't discuss this with any other group, but make a bee-line for 'your' space, overcoming any obstacles in the way.
- When you arrive in the place you have chosen, find a way of making it your space (e.g. put chairs round it in order to keep people out, put a notice up, or just stand guard over it). Now sing a song which everyone in your group knows, ignoring the others.
- Ephesians 2 vv. 11–21 is read.
- Welcome another group into fellowship, sharing your space with them. If they are already starting to share with someone else, do so as well, until the space only contains one lot of people.
- See how much you can find which you all have in common. Choose an experience which everyone recognizes and build up a group representation of this.
- Form into a long line by standing behind someone and putting your hands on their shoulders; move round the space, going in and out of chairs and furniture.
- Holding hands in a circle, say the 'peace prayer' together:
  'Lead us from death to life, from falsehood to truth
  Lead us from despair to hope, from fear to trust
  Lead us from hate to love, from war to peace.
  Let peace fill our hearts, our world, our universe,
  Peace, peace, peace.'
- After a time of open prayer, say 'Our Father' together
- Say goodbye to everyone individually.

This is an oblique, but powerful, way of dealing with a pressing human problem – perhaps the most stubborn and persistent difficulty faced by Christians. The need to transcend every kind of human division is central to our faith. Peter's roof-top vision could be taken as the definitive statement of the Church's attitude: "What God has made clean, you must not call profane" (Acts 10 v 15) Christ has redeemed all of creation, not simply the parts we may approve of. Five thousand years later, and we still need telling! . . .

10. Growing as Christ's Body
A

- Psalm 92
- Introduce a Liturgical theme:
  (*See Workshop* 1).
- Sing a Hymn/Song

B

- Wander around the space by yourself. You don't need to avoid other people, whom you may greet in passing – but only if they appear to want to acknowledge *you*.
- When the Leader gives a sign to do so, sit or stand somewhere by yourself, still keeping your distance.
- On a sign from the Leader, move across to sit near someone else, (or join a pair who have already done this).
- When the music starts, start moving with it, first of all keeping your distance from other couples and groups; then as the music begins to swell in volume, more closer and closer to the centre of the room, until you are all within reach of one another. Reach out and take someone's hand.
- Now stand together in as tight a circle as you can manage. Put your arms round one another's shoulders, swaying to the music.
- Two members of the group, one younger than the other, read Ephesians 4 vv. 1–16 (1–10, 11–16)
- Dance together as a group, sometimes by yourself, sometimes with someone else, taking in the whole group so that your movement embraces the entire space and everybody in it. (If you find this kind of movement out of the question, encourage the more mobile to dance round you, so that you aren't excluded from the dance in any way).
- Now sit down in a circle together. As Holy Spirit moves you, pray aloud or silently, responding to the spoken prayers with "Amen: Christ be praised".

- Say 'Our Father' together.
- Holding hands, enjoy a time of silence together; then gently squeeze your neighbour's hand, and say goodbye.
- When Leader gives a sign, say, in chorus, "Amen: Christ be praised". (as loudly as possible!)

This is a celebration of what has already taken place, of course. Human beings – even members of church congregations – have difficulty in coming to terms with their own spiritual identities and need help sometimes in taking Christ personally, tending either to think too much, ending up prisoners of their own logic, or not enough, in which case they run the risk of losing sight of the sheer unlikeliness of what has happened to them! They need to be reminded from time to time of their incorporation with 'the whole Christ' and what this means for them and the rest of the congregation. This workshop may be a way of doing this.

Bibliography

Anglican Liturgical Commission (2000) *Common Worship*, London: Church House Publishing.

Boorg, M. ter (2007) "Implicit Religion in Holland: A Silent March, Football Mania and a Pop-funeral Manifestation", paper read at *NSIRCS* Denton Conference, Denton. May 2007.

Buber, M. (1957) *Pointing the Way*, London: Routledge.

Buber, M. (1961) *Between Man and Man*, London: Collins.

Butcher, S. H. (1951) *Aristotle's Theory of Poetry and Fine Art*, New York: Dover.

Carroll, L. (1876) *The Hunting of the Snark*, London: Macmillan.

Cullman, O. (1953) *Early Christian Worship*, London: SCM.

Davies, J. G. (1972) *A Dictionary of Liturgy and Worship*, London: SCM.

Eliade, M. (1955) *The Myth of the Eternal Return*, London: Sheed & Ward.

Eliade, M. (1963) *Rites and Symbols of Initiation*, New York: Harper & Row.

Erikson, E. (1985) *The Life Cycle Completed*, New York: Norton.

Freud, S. (1907) "Obsessive Actions and Religious Practices" in *Standard Edition of the Works of Sigmund Freud IX* (1953–1974), London: Hogarth Press & Institute of Psychoanalysis.

Fulghum, R. (1995) *From Beginning to End: The Rituals of our Lives*, London: Rider.

Gennep, A. van *The Rites of Passage* (trans. M. B. Vizedom & C. L. Cafee), London: Routledge.

Gergen, M. & K. (2003) *Social Construction: A Reader*, London: Sage.

Gorman, C. (1972) *The Book of Ceremony*, Cambridge: Whole Earth Tools.

Grainger, R. (1988a) *The Unburied*, Worthing: Churchman.

Grainger, R (1988b) *The Message of the Rite*, Cambridge: Lutterworth.

Grainger, R. (1998) *The Social Symbolism of Grief and Mourning*, London: Kingsley.

Graham, E. (1994) "Truth or Dare? Sexuality, Liturgy and Pastoral Theology", in D. Williams & J. Swinton (eds) *Spiritual Dimensions of Pastoral Care*, London: Kingsley (2001).

Kavanagh, A. (1982) *Elements of Rite*, Collegeville: Pueblo.

Lahad, M. (1994) "What is Dramatherapy?", in S. Jennings, A. Cattenach, S. Mitchell, A. Chesner & B. Meldrum, *The Handbook of Dramatherapy*, London: Routledge (1994).

Langley, D. (2006) *An Introduction to Dramatherapy*, London: Sage.

Leeuw, G. van der *Religion in Essence and Manifestation*, London: Allen & Unwin.

Levinas, E. (1969) *Totality and Infinity: An Essay in Exteriority* (trans. A. Lingus), Pittsburgh: Duquesne University Press.

Levinas, E. (1987) *Time and the Other* (trans. R. A. Cohen), Pittsburgh: Duquesne University Press.

Levy-Strauss, C. (1969) *Totemism*, Harmondsworth: Penguin.

Marcel, G. (1965) *Being and Having*, London: Collins.

Mauss, M. & Hubert, H. (1909) *Mélanges d'Histoire des Réligions*, Paris.

McCabe, H. (1964) *The New Creation*, London: Sheed & Ward.

McGuire, W. & Hull, R. F. C. (1978) *Jung Speaking*, London: Thames & Hudson.

Noakes, K. W. (1979) "Initiation, from New Testament Times to St Cyprian" in C. Jones, G. Wainwright & E. Arnold (eds), *The Study of Liturgy*, London: SPCK (1979).

Ricoeur, P. (1971) "What is a Text? Explanation and Interpretation" in D. Rasmussen, *Mythic, Symbolic and Philosophical Anthropology*, The Hague: Nijhoff.

Sarbin, T. R. (1986) *Narrative Psychology*, New York: Praeger.

Scheff, T. (1979) *Catharsis in Drama, Healing and Ritual*, Berkeley: University of California Press.

Stuart, E. (ed.) (1992) *Daring to Speak Love's Name: A Gay and Lesbian Prayer Book*, London: Hamish Hamilton.

Thornton, L. (1963) *The Common Life in the Body of Christ*, London: Dacre.

Turner, V. (1974) *The Ritual Process*, Harmondsworth: Penguin.

Williams, C. (1957) *Descent into Hell*, London: Faber & Faber.

Winnicott, D. W. (1971) *Playing and Reality*, London: Tavistock.

Zizioulas, J. (1985) *Being as Communion*, SVS Press.

Index